Ready, Set, Go!®

MW01093001

MCAS

English Language Arts

Grade 10

Staff of Research & Education Association

Research & Education Association

The Curriculum Framework Standards in this book were created and implemented by the Massachusetts Board of Education. For further information, visit the Department of Education website at *http://www.doe.mass.edu/mcas/*.

Research & Education Association
61 Ethel Road West
Piscataway, New Jersey 08854
E-mail: info@rea.com

Ready, Set, Go!®
Massachusetts MCAS English Language Arts, Grade 10

Published 2009

Copyright © 2007 by Research & Education Association, Inc.

Printed in the United States of America

Library of Congress Control Number 2006930578

ISBN-13: 978-0-7386-0190-8
ISBN-10: 0-7386-0190-X

REA® and *Ready, Set, Go!*® are registered trademarks of Research & Education Association, Inc.

Contents

Section 1: Reading

Section 2: Writing

About Research & Education Association

Founded in 1959, Research & Education Association is dedicated to publishing the finest and most effective educational materials—including software, study guides, and test preps—for students in middle school, high school, college, graduate school, and beyond. Today, REA's wide-ranging catalog is a leading resource for teachers, students, and professionals. We invite you to visit us at *www.rea.com* to find out how REA is making the world smarter.

Acknowledgments

We would like to thank REA's Larry B. Kling, Vice President, Editorial, for supervising development; Pam Weston, Vice President, Publishing, for setting the quality standards for production integrity and managing the publication to completion; Christine Reilley, Senior Editor, for project management and preflight editorial review; Diane Goldschmidt, Senior Editor, for post-production quality assurance; Barbara McGowran for copyediting the manuscript; Terry Casey for indexing; Christine Saul, Senior Graphic Artist, for cover design; and Jeff LoBalbo, Senior Graphic Artist, for post-production file mapping.

We also gratefully acknowledge the writers, educators, and editors of REA and Northeast Editing for content development and Matrix Publishing for page design and typesetting.

Introduction

About This Book

This book provides you with an accurate and complete representation of the English Language Arts (ELA) portion of the Massachusetts Comprehensive Assessment System (MCAS). The ELA portion of the MCAS includes two sections: Composition, during which you will create a composition in response to a writing prompt, and Language and Literature, during which you will answer a series of multiple-choice and open-response questions based on various reading selections. The reviews in this book are designed to provide the information and strategies you need to do well on both sections of the test. The two practice tests in the book are based on the MCAS and contain questions exactly like those you can expect to encounter on the official test. Following each practice test is an answer key with detailed explanations designed to help you completely understand the test material.

About the Test

Who Takes the Test and What Is It Used For?

The MCAS is given to public school students throughout Massachusetts to measure performance based on the learning standards in the *Massachusetts Curriculum Frameworks*. The two sections of the ELA portion of the MCAS are Composition, which tests students on the *Frameworks'* Composition strand, and Language and Literature, which tests students on the Language and Reading and Literature strands. The results of both sections of the ELA portion of the MCAS allow parents, students, and educators to follow student progress; identify strengths, weaknesses, and gaps in curriculum and instruction; fine-tune curriculum alignment with statewide standards; gather diagnostic information that can be used to improve student performance; and identify students who may need additional support services or remediation. In addition, each student must pass the ELA portion of the tenth-grade MCAS as one requirement toward receiving a high school diploma.

Is There a Registration Fee?

No. Because all Massachusetts public high school students are required to take the MCAS and pass the test to receive a high school diploma, no fee is required.

Test Accommodations and Special Situations

Every effort is made to provide a level playing field for students with disabilities taking the MCAS and seeking a standard high school diploma. For purposes of the MCAS, a student with a disability has either an Individualized Education Program (IEP) provided under the Individuals with Disabilities Education Act or a plan provided under Section 504 of the Rehabilitation Act of 1973. A student's IEP team or 504 team must determine annually how the student with a disability will participate in the MCAS in each subject scheduled for assessment. This information must be documented in the student's IEP and should be documented in the student's 504 plan. The team may determine that the student can take the standard test with or without accommodations or may be eligible to take the MCAS Alternate Assessment.

All students with limited English proficiency (LEP) must participate in all MCAS tests scheduled for their grades, regardless of the number of years they have been in the United States. The only exception is for LEP students who are in their first year of enrollment in U.S. schools. These students are not required to participate in the English Language Arts tests. Any student who is or has been an LEP student may use an approved bilingual word-to-word dictionary on MCAS tests.

In addition to participating in the MCAS, LEP students must annually take the Massachusetts English Proficiency Assessment (MEPA) tests in reading, writing, speaking, and listening.

Additional Information and Support

These additional resources will help you prepare to take the MCAS:

- The official MCAS Web site at *http://www.doe.mass.edu/mcas/*
- The Massachusetts Department of Education Web site at *http://www.doe.mass.edu*

How to Use This Book

What Do I Study First?

Read the suggestions for test taking in this chapter and the review sections (Chapters 2 through 8). Studying the review sections thoroughly will reinforce the basic skills you need to do well on the test. Be sure to take the practice tests to become familiar with the format and procedures involved with taking the actual MCAS.

When Should I Start Studying?

It is never too early to start studying for the MCAS. The earlier you begin, the more time you will have to sharpen your skills. Do not procrastinate! Cramming is *not* an effective way to study because it does not allow you the time you need to learn the test material. The sooner you learn the format of the exam, the more time you will have to familiarize yourself with the exam content.

Format of the English Language Arts Portion of the MCAS

Overview of the ELA Portion of the MCAS

The ELA portion of the MCAS is designed to test students' ability to read and write, knowledge of basic literary concepts, and familiarity with basic writing strategies. The Composition portion of the MCAS includes one writing prompt, and the Language and Literature portion includes thirty-six multiple-choice questions and four open-response items.

The following types of passages are included on MCAS:

Short stories	Editorials
Novel excerpts	Interviews
Poetry	Letters
Plays	Diary entries
Myths, legends, fables	Newspaper articles
Biographies, autobiographies	Reviews
Essays	Instructions
Speeches	Advertisements

Scoring the Tests

Each multiple-choice question on the Language and Literature portion of the MCAS has only one correct answer. Therefore, these items are machine-scored.

Open-response questions require students to generate, rather than recognize, their responses. Students create a one- or two-paragraph response in writing or in the form of a narrative or a chart, table, diagram, illustration, or graph, as appropriate. Students can respond correctly using various strategies and approaches.

Responses to open-response questions are scored using a scoring guide, or rubric, for each question. The scoring guide indicates what knowledge and skills students must demonstrate to earn 1, 2, 3, or 4 score points. Answers to open-response questions are not scored for spelling, punctuation, or grammar. Responses are scored by one scorer at grades 3 through 8 and high school and by two scorers independently at grade 10.

Writing prompts included on the MCAS Composition test require students to respond by creating a written composition. Student compositions are scored independently by two scorers based on the following:

- Topic development, based on a six-point scale, with students receiving from 2 to 12 points (the sum of the scores from each of the two scorers)

- Standard English conventions, based on a four-point scale, with students receiving from 2 to 8 points (the sum of the scores from each of the two scorers)

Test-Taking Strategies

What to Do Before the Test

- Pay attention in class.

- Carefully work through the review sections of this book. Mark any topics that you find difficult so you can focus on them while studying and get extra help if necessary.

- Take the practice tests and become familiar with the format of the MCAS. When you are practicing, simulate the conditions under which you will be taking the actual test. Stay calm and pace yourself. After simulating the test only a couple of times, you will feel more confident, and this will boost your chances of doing well.

- If you have difficulty concentrating or taking tests in general, you may have severe test anxiety. Tell your parents, a teacher, a counselor, the school nurse, or a school psychologist well in advance of the test. They may be able to suggest some useful strategies to help you feel more relaxed so that you can do your best on the test.

What to Do During the Test

- Read all the possible answers. Just because you think you have found the correct response, do not automatically assume that it is the best answer. Read through each answer choice to be sure you are not making a mistake by jumping to conclusions.

- Use the process of elimination. Go through each answer to a question and eliminate as many of the answer choices as possible. By eliminating two answer choices, you will give yourself a better chance of getting the item correct because there will only be two choices left.

- Work quickly and steadily and avoid focusing on any one question for too long. Taking the practice tests in this book will help you learn to budget your time on the actual test.

- Work on the easiest questions first. If you find yourself working too long on one question, make a mark next to it on your test booklet and go on to the next question. After you have answered all the questions that you know, go back to the ones you skipped.

- Be sure that the answer oval you are marking corresponds to the number of the question in the test booklet. Because the multiple-choice sections are graded by machine, marking one wrong answer can throw off your answer key and your score. Be extremely careful.

- Work from the answer choices. You can use a multiple-choice format to your advantage by working backward from the answer choices to answer the question. You may be able to make an educated guess based on eliminating choices that you know do not fit the question.

Standard Breakdown by Chapter*

Chapters	Standards
Chapter 1: Vocabulary and Language, Part 1	Standard 4: Students will understand and acquire new vocabulary and use it correctly in reading and writing.
	4.23 Identify and use correctly idioms, cognates, words with literal and figurative meanings, and patterns of word changes that indicate different meanings or functions.
	4.24 Use knowledge of Greek, Latin, and Norse mythology, the Bible, and other works often alluded to in British and American literature to understand the meanings of new words.
	Standard 5: Students will analyze Standard English grammar and usage and recognize how its vocabulary has developed and been influenced by other languages.
	5.26 Analyze the structure of a sentence.
	Standard 6: Students will describe, analyze, and use appropriately formal and informal English.
	6.8 Identify content-specific vocabulary, terminology, or jargon unique to particular social or professional groups.
Chapter 2: Vocabulary and Language, Part 2	Standard 15: Students will identify and analyze how an author's words appeal to the senses, create imagery, suggest mood, and set tone and provide evidence from the text to support their understanding.
	15.7 Evaluate how an author's choice of words advances the theme or purpose of a work.
	15.8 Identify and describe the importance of sentence variety in the overall effectiveness of an imaginary/ literary or informational/expository work.

* The Curriculum Framework Standards in this table were created and implemented by the Massachusetts Board of Education. For further information, visit the Board of Education website at *www.doe.mass.edu/mcas/*.

Chapters	Standards
Chapter 3: Main Idea and Supporting Details	Standard 8: Students will identify the basic facts and main ideas in a text and use them as the basis for interpretation.
	Fiction:
	8.29 Identify and analyze patterns of imagery or symbolism.
	8.30 Identify and interpret themes and give supporting evidence from a text.
	Nonfiction:
	8.31 Analyze the logic and use of evidence in an author's argument.
Chapter 4: Short Stories	Standard 11: Students will identify, analyze, and apply knowledge of theme in a literary work and provide evidence from the text to support their understanding.
	11.5 Apply knowledge of the concept that the theme or meaning of a selection represents a view or comment on life, and provide support from the text for the identified theme.
	Standard 12: Students will identify, analyze, and apply knowledge of the structure and elements of fiction and provide evidence from the text to support their understanding.
	12.5 Locate and analyze such elements in fiction as point of view, foreshadowing, and irony.

Chapters	Standards
Chapter 5: Poetry	Standard 14: Students will identify, analyze, and apply knowledge of the theme, structure, and elements of poetry and provide evidence from the text to support their understanding. 14.5 Identify, respond to, and analyze the effects of sound, form, figurative language, graphics, and dramatic structure of poems: Sound (alliteration, onomatopoeia, rhyme scheme, consonance, assonance) Form (ballad, sonnet, heroic couplets) Figurative language (personification, metaphor, simile, hyperbole, symbolism) Dramatic structure
Chapter 6: Myths, Classical Literature, and Drama	Standard 16: Students will identify, analyze, and apply knowledge of the themes, structure, and elements of myths, traditional narratives, and classical literature and provide evidence from the text to support their understanding. 16.11 Analyze the characters, structure, and themes of classical Greek drama and epic poetry. Standard 17: Students will identify, analyze, and apply knowledge of the themes, structure, and elements of drama and provide evidence from the text to support their understanding. 17.7 Identify and analyze how dramatic conventions support, interpret, and enhance dramatic text.
Chapter 7: Nonfiction	Standard 13: Students will identify, analyze, and apply knowledge of the purpose, structure, and elements of nonfiction or informational materials and provide evidence from the text to support their understanding. 13.24 Analyze the logic and use of evidence in an author's argument. 13.25 Analyze and explain the structure and elements of nonfiction works.

Chapters	Standards
Chapter 8: Composition	Standard 19: Students will write with a clear focus, coherent organization, and sufficient detail.
	19.30 Write coherent compositions with a clear focus, objective presentation of alternate views, rich detail, well-developed paragraphs, and logical argumentation.
	Standard 20: Students will write for different audiences and purposes.
	20.5 Use different levels of formality, style, and tone when composing for different audiences.
	Standard 21: Students will demonstrate improvement in organization, content, paragraph, development, level of detail, style, tone, and word choice (diction) in their compositions after revising them.
	21.8 Revise writing by attending to topic/idea development, organization, level of detail, language/style, sentence structure, grammar and usage, and mechanics.
	Standard 22: Students will use knowledge of Standard English conventions in their writing, revising, and editing.
	22.9 Use knowledge of types of clauses (main and subordinate), verbals (gerunds, infinitives, participles), mechanics (semicolons, colons, hyphens), usage (tense consistency), sentence structure (parallel structure), and standard English spelling when writing and editing.
	Standard 23: Students will organize ideas in writing in a way that makes sense for their purpose.
	23.9 Integrate the use of organizing techniques that break up strict chronological order in a story (starting in the middle of the action, then filling in background information using flashbacks). For example, after reading the short story, "The Bet," by Anton Chekhov, students use flashbacks in their own stories and discuss the effect of this technique.
	23.10 Organize information into a coherent essay or report with a thesis statement in the introduction, transition sentences to link paragraphs, and a conclusion.

Chapter 1

Vocabulary and Language, Part 1

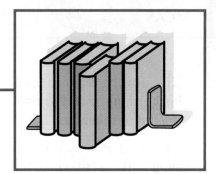

Standard 4: Students will understand and acquire new vocabulary and use it correctly in reading and writing.

    4.23 Identify and use correctly idioms, cognates, words with literal and figurative meanings, and patterns of word changes that indicate different meanings or functions.

    4.24 Use knowledge of Greek, Latin, and Norse mythology, the Bible, and other works often alluded to in British and American literature to understand the meanings of new words.

Standard 5: Students will analyze Standard English grammar and usage and recognize how its vocabulary has developed and been influenced by other languages.

    5.26 Analyze the structure of a sentence.

Standard 6: Students will describe, analyze, and use appropriately formal and informal English.

    6.8 Identify content-specific vocabulary, terminology, or jargon unique to particular social or professional groups.

Context Clues

You will be asked vocabulary questions on the MCAS. These questions most often ask you to define a word used in a passage. You can often figure out a word's meaning by looking at the context of the word—that is, the words and sentences around it. Consider this example:

Kirk was a huge hunk of a dog. When standing upright on his hind legs, he could easily rest his front paws on a man's shoulders. His enormous presence scared most passersby when Kirk strolled in the park on his daily walk on the leash. Other dogs, too, shunned

1

Kirk, fearing death or severe injury should Kirk decide to clamp down on their flesh with his crushing jaws. No one had reason to worry, however. Terrified of squirrels and distrustful of robins and butterflies, Kirk was the most **docile** dog in the world.

Use the context of this passage to determine the meaning of the word *docile*. Write the meaning of the word on the line below.

You should be able to tell from the context that *docile* means *gentle* or *kind*.

Words with Multiple Meanings

Some questions on the MCAS will ask you about words used in such a way that their meaning is not literal. Some of these words or phrases might be idioms—expressions that are natural to people from a particular area or part of the world. For example, have you ever called someone a "backseat driver"? If so, you used an idiom—the person is not really driving from the backseat of the car but instead is acting like an authority on driving by telling the driver what to do. Another idiom is "go back to square one," which you may have used to describe your starting an assignment over.

Cognates are words that have a common origin, meaning they derived from the same word. For example, consider the Proto-Indo-European word *nekwt*, which refers to the time of day when the sun goes down. In English, this word is *night*. In Scottish, this word is *nicht*. *Night* and *nicht* are cognates of *nekwt*. Although cognates do not always have the same meaning, they often do. On the MCAS, you may be able to determine the meaning of a word that is a cognate to a word in the English language simply by analyzing the context.

Some questions on the MCAS might ask you to identify words in a passage that are jargon—that is, words related to a particular field. What do you think of when you hear the words *mouse, keyboard, drive,* and *printer*? These words are jargon related to computers.

Parts of a Sentence

Although much less common than questions on vocabulary words, some MCAS questions will ask you to identify a word's part of speech. For example, you might be asked, "What part of speech is the word *buckle* in paragraph 1?" The word *buckle* can be a noun or a verb—think about a belt buckle and buckling your shoe. To correctly answer these questions, you should go back and reread the word in the sentence. Remember that nouns come before or after verbs, which describe the action in a sentence. Adjectives modify nouns, and adverbs modify verbs.

Passage 1

Read the following passage. Then answer the questions that follow. Use the Tip below each question to help you choose the correct answer. When you finish, read the answer explanations at the end of this chapter.

Excerpt from *Wuthering Heights*
by Emily Brontë

1 Yesterday afternoon set in misty and cold. I had half a mind to spend it by my study fire, instead of wading through heath and mud to Wuthering Heights. On coming up from dinner, however, (N.B.—I dine between twelve and one o'clock; the housekeeper, a matronly lady, taken as a fixture along with the house, could not, or would not, comprehend my request that I might be served at five)—on mounting the stairs with this lazy intention, and stepping into the room, I saw a servant-girl on her knees surrounded by brushes and coal-scuttles, and raising an infernal dust as she extinguished the flames with heaps of cinders. This spectacle drove me back immediately; I took my hat, and, after a four-miles' walk, arrived at Heathcliff's garden-gate just in time to escape the first feathery flakes of a snow-shower.

2 On that bleak hill-top the earth was hard with a black frost, and the air made me shiver through every limb. Being unable to remove the chain, I jumped over, and, running up the flagged causeway bordered with straggling gooseberry-bushes, knocked vainly for admittance, till my knuckles tingled and the dogs howled.

3 "Wretched inmates!" I ejaculated, mentally, "you deserve perpetual isolation from your species for your churlish inhospitality. At least, I would not keep my doors barred in the day-time. I don't care—I will get in!"

❓ Questions

1   Which of the following is **closest** in meaning to the word *infernal* as it is used in paragraph 1?

    A   stifling

    B   foul smelling

    C   choking

    D   deadly

 Carefully consider each answer choice. Remember that the girl put out the flames with heaps—large amounts—of cinder. *Stifling* implies that the dust might be hot. While *deadly* seems like the right answer, do you think the girl died from the dust? Do you think the dust had an odor? Or, do you think the dust made the girl cough?

2   In paragraph 3, what does the word *churlish* mean?

    A   exceptional

    B   frequent

    C   impolite

    D   strange

 What can you tell about the "inmates" from the way the narrator describes them? Were they nice to her? Do you think they act in a way that is socially acceptable? Select the answer choice that best tells what she thinks of their inhospitality.

3   What part of speech is the word *walk* in paragraph 1?

    A   verb

    B   noun

    C   adjective

    D   adverb

 The narrator says that she arrived at Heathcliff's gate after a four-mile walk. In this instance, the word *walk* means *distance*. What part of speech is distance?

Passage 2

Read the following passage. Then answer the questions that follow. Use the Tip below each question to help you choose the correct answer. When you finish, read the answer explanations at the end of this chapter.

The Six Nations of the Iroquois

1   Long before the United States of America was created, a group of American Indians known as the Iroquois formed a united government of their own. Their government was known as the Six Nations of the Iroquois. It was so fair and effective that it helped to inspire the creation of the United States in 1776.

2   The history of the Iroquois reaches back thousands of years. Since ancient times, many American Indian tribes lived in the lands around New York State. Among them were the Mohawk, Seneca, Onondaga, Oneida, and Cayuga. These five tribes had been at odds with one another for many years. A mysterious man arrived in their lands with a plan for peace. Representatives of the five tribes met and listened to the words of their eloquent visitor. After that, they decided to make peace and unite into a single government. Later a sixth tribe, the Tuscarora, joined the group.

3   The government formed by the group of tribes was called the Six Nations, and immediately it proved its worth. The six tribes no longer had to waste time and energy fighting with one another. Instead, they could advance their cultures and defend themselves against common enemies. Among them, the Six Nations controlled much of the land of the northeast. They referred to their shared lands as their Longhouse. They stationed powerful tribes to guard each end of it. By the 1600s, the Six Nations was a force to be reckoned with.

4   Colonists from Britain and France began gathering in North America. The Iroquois were pressed into making treaties and agreements with them. Although strictly honest in their dealings, the Iroquois understandably felt no deep loyalty to either the British or the French. The colonists from both countries were frequently unfair and often brutal to the American Indians and took much of their lands. The Iroquois created a kind of survival technique that involved playing the British and French against one another. By keeping the Europeans angry with one another, the Iroquois could gain benefits and keep more of their power.

5   However, the Iroquois could not maintain their "catbird seat" between the European competitors for long. As the British and French began to fight one another, the Iroquois were drawn in and forced to choose sides. Later, during the Revolutionary War, they were again forced to choose. This time, they had to decide whether to join the British or the Americans. The Six Nations became desegregated during these wars. By around 1800, the power of the Iroquois was broken.

6   Although the Americans, the newcomers to the continent, claimed control over the land, the Iroquois people never died out. Descendants of the Iroquois groups that supported the Americans in the Revolution live today as U.S. citizens. They mostly live on reservations in New York State, Oklahoma, and Wisconsin. Many thousands of other Iroquois people live in Canada today. These people are the descendants of Iroquois who supported the British.

7   The lands that were originally home to the Iroquois are now used by people who are not Native Americans. These lands have been changed greatly from their natural state. Today they are largely covered in highways, railroads, reservoirs, power lines, and other technologies. Ironically, most modern Iroquois reservations have not been given the benefits of such helpful projects. Because of this, the standard of living in Iroquois reservations is usually lower than the communities around them.

8   Despite this, Iroquois reservations are not crude or primitive places. Like most communities, they respect the symbols and customs of their ancestors, but they have not been "left behind" in the past. Most reservations today are fully modernized. Some visitors expect to see ancient shelters like teepees and wigwams still in use. These visitors are surprised to realize that most modern Iroquois live in frame or manufactured housing.

9   Many reservations are full of small businesses. These include markets, mills, repair shops, and gas stations. The communities also support banks, libraries, sports arenas, museums, cultural centers, and places of worship. Gaming is a major industry among some Indian groups. Tourists from all over the United States visit reservations to try their luck at casinos and bingo halls.

10   The other major industry, one that provides a link between modern Iroquois and their ancient ancestry, is art. The crafts of the Iroquois are unique and generate increasing interest as the world becomes more reliant on bland manufactured items. Craftspeople among the American Indians carry on long, proud traditions and skills. They are masters of beadwork, basket and doll making, and pottery.

11   Much of this art is purchased by tourists, and that helps the economy of the reservations. It also allows Iroquois artists to spread their talents to other communities. Additionally, Iroquois artwork is featured in many museums and at cultural festivals. Other forms of art, including music, dancing, and storytelling, are also popular among modern Indians.

12   Despite the great changes and suffering among the Iroquois, the Six Nations is still very much alive. Today, Iroquois communities still select chiefs to represent them at the on-going meetings of the Iroquois Counsel. The Six Nations considers itself independent from the control of the U.S. and Canadian governments. The leaders and citizens of the Six Nations continue to work hard to benefit their people and preserve their customs into the future.

? Questions

4   What does the author mean by saying in paragraph 5 that the Six Nations *desegregated*?

   A   came into conflict with

   B   pulled apart from

   C   were conquered by

   D   became concerned with

 TIP   Even if you think you know the meaning of the word *desegregated*, go back and reread paragraph 5. Look at the way the word is used in the sentence. Note that the Iroquois lost their power because they desegregated.

5   In paragraph 8, what does the word *modernized* mean?

   A   practical

   B   superficial

   C   up-to-date

   D   simplified

 TIP   Consider the word as it is used in context. You might also want to consider the meaning of the root word, *modern*. These considerations will give you clues as to what the answer might be.

6   What part of speech is the word *advance* in paragraph 3?

   A   noun

   B   verb

   C   adjective

   D   noun

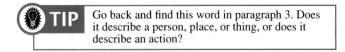

TIP   Go back and find this word in paragraph 3. Does it describe a person, place, or thing, or does it describe an action?

7   What is the best meaning of *bland* as it is used in paragraph 10?

   A   tasteless

   B   plain

   C   cheap

   D   common

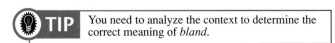

TIP   You need to analyze the context to determine the correct meaning of *bland*.

Passage 3

Read the following poem. Then answer the questions that follow. Use the Tip below each question to help you choose the correct answer. When you finish, read the answer explanations at the end of this chapter.

Annabel Lee
by Edgar Allan Poe

1   It was many and many a year ago,

    In a kingdom by the sea,

    That a maiden there lived whom you may know

    By the name of Annabel Lee;

    And this maiden she lived with no other thought

    Than to love and be loved by me.

2   *She* was a child and *I* was a child,

    In this kingdom by the sea:

    But we loved with a love that was more than love—

    I and my Annabel Lee;

    With a love that the winged seraphs of Heaven

    Coveted her and me.

3   And this was the reason that, long ago,

    In this kingdom by the sea,

    A wind blew out of a cloud by night

    Chilling my Annabel Lee;

    So that her highborn kinsmen came

    And bore her away from me,

    To shut her up in a sepulchre

    In this kingdom by the sea.

4   The angels, not half so happy in Heaven,

      Went envying her and me—

      Yes! that was the reason (as all men know,

      In this kingdom by the sea)

      That the wind came out of the cloud, chilling

      And killing my Annabel Lee.

5   But our love it was stronger by far than the love

      Of those who were older than we—

      Of many far wiser than we—

      And neither the angels in Heaven above,

      Nor the demons down under the sea,

      Can ever dissever my soul from the soul

      Of the beautiful Annabel Lee:—

6   For the moon never beams without bringing me dreams

      Of the beautiful Annabel Lee;

      And the stars never rise but I see the bright eyes

      Of the beautiful Annabel Lee;

      And so, all the night-tide, I lie down by the side

      Of my darling, my darling, my life and my bride,

      In her sepulchre there by the sea—

      In her tomb by the side of the sea.

❓ Questions

8   Which of the following **best** describes the meaning of *coveted* in stanza 2?

   A   moved

   B   wanted

   C   loved

   D   watched

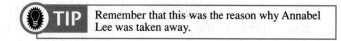

TIP   Remember that this was the reason why Annabel Lee was taken away.

9   What part of speech is *chilling* in stanza 3?

   A   noun

   B   adjective

   C   verb

   D   adverb

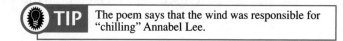

TIP   The poem says that the wind was responsible for "chilling" Annabel Lee.

10   What is the meaning of *dissever* as it used in the fifth stanza of the poem?

   A   separate

   B   forget

   C   remarry

   D   confuse

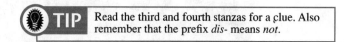

TIP   Read the third and fourth stanzas for a clue. Also remember that the prefix *dis-* means *not*.

Passage 4

Read the following passage. Then answer the questions that follow. Use the Tip below each question to help you choose the correct answer. When you finish, read the answer explanations at the end of this chapter.

Curious Crop Circles

1   Imagine, for a moment, that you are a farmer. One morning you awaken to find a large circular pattern in the middle of your fields. Where rows of wheat, soy, or corn stood tall just yesterday, there is now a perfectly shaped circle. For many farmers around the world, this is a baffling reality. This strange phenomenon is known as crop circles, and they are characterized by the symmetrical flattening of crops into a geometric pattern, usually occurring overnight when there are no witnesses. The formations generally appear starting in late spring until early autumn, with most circles being discovered during the summer months. The United Kingdom has had the largest number of crop circles over the years, but countries like the United States, Germany, Canada, and the Netherlands have reported an increase in incidents since the late twentieth century.

2   Crop circles first garnered international attention in the media during the early 1980s, when a series of circles where discovered in southern England. However, many argue that crop circles have been reported since the early seventeenth century. A tale dating back to 1678 tells of a farmer who refused to pay a laborer to mow a field. That night, the field appeared to

be on fire. When the farmer went to inspect his crops the following morning, instead of finding charred remains, he discovered that the field had indeed been mowed—but by whom or what he could not say. Although many dispute the validity of this early incident, others note that farmers have been reporting crop circles for generations.

3   Of course, the real mystery is who or what is behind the creation of these circles that appear in the middle of the night. Theories explaining the existence of crop circles range from the mundane to the supernatural. Many feel that most crop circles are merely elaborate hoaxes perpetrated by people who have nothing better to do with their time or are looking for their fifteen minutes of fame.

4   Two of the most famous hoaxers were discovered in England. In 1991, Doug Bower and Dave Chorley claimed that they had been staging crop circles for nearly fifteen years, creating more than 200 circles. The men said they would sneak into fields at night and, using a wooden plank tied to some string, would flatten the crops into circles while the owners of the fields were asleep. Although Bower and Chorley may have been telling the truth, their actions do not account for the more than two thousand other circles that were reported around the country during the time the two men were working.

5   Today the debate over hoaxing continues. Professional circle makers have appeared on numerous television programs, trying to prove that crop circles, even the extremely complex ones, are made by people. Circle makers have created formations for everything from music videos to movies, like the 2002 film *Signs*. Several businesses have used computer technology to create circle advertisements in fields where airplane passengers are most likely to spot them.

6   Still, crop circle researchers note several key differences between artificial and what they call authentic crop circles. First, researchers note that when an artificial pattern is formed, there is usually evidence of a human presence left behind, like footprints in the soil or impressions from the tools that were used. Second, when a genuine formation is found, there is sometimes unexplainable effects on the environment that do not occur when a circle is the work of tricksters.

7   One especially interesting fact that researchers point out is that crops that are particularly unyielding, like canola plants, tend to snap when they are bent by the tools that many hoaxers use, whereas these same crops inexplicably bend in "legitimate" formations. Other important differences that researchers have noted between what they feel are real crop circles and hoaxes are cellular changes in plants, changes in plants' seeds, and dehydrated soil in genuine cases.

8   The most popular, and the most controversial, idea behind the cause of crop circles is that they are the work of extraterrestrial life forms trying to make contact with human beings. Proponents of this idea believe that the formations must be created by an intelligent life form and that the circles are far too intricate for even a small team of humans to create overnight without being caught. To support this claim, many people point to other strange phenomena that sometimes accompany crop circles as evidence of an alien presence. These reports in-

clude seeing balls of light and hearing unusual sounds in the areas where the circles are later discovered. Some believe that this theory might also explain the curious effect that some circles have on plants, but so far there is not enough conclusive evidence to link crop circles to an otherworldly force.

9 The search for a more terrestrial answer to the cause of crop circles continues. Some scientists believe that the earth itself is the cause of these mysterious events. One argument is that a shift in the earth's electromagnetic field would be enough to flatten crops without breaking them. Another idea is that changes in the planet's weather patterns over the last few centuries could be the source of crop circles. Several other theories conclude that crop circles are probably more natural than supernatural.

10 Although some crop circle cases have proved to be nothing more than pranks, others are not so easy to dismiss. Until there is a clear-cut explanation for the phenomena, these mysterious formations will likely continue to fascinate researchers and the public worldwide for some time to come.

? Questions

11 What is the meaning of the word *baffling* in paragraph 1?

A   interesting

B   terrifying

C   exciting

D   confusing

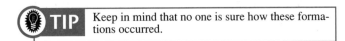 **TIP** Keep in mind that no one is sure how these formations occurred.

12 Which of the following best describes the meaning of *garnered* in paragraph 2?

A   accepted

B   attracted

C   published

D   requested

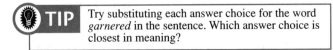 **TIP** Try substituting each answer choice for the word *garnered* in the sentence. Which answer choice is closest in meaning?

13 What is the meaning of the word *mundane* in paragraph 3?

   A strange

   B exceptional

   C easy

   D boring

 TIP Notice that the sentence says that the circles range from the mundane to the supernatural. You can tell from this context that supernatural is the opposite extreme of mundane.

14 What part of speech is the word *contact* in paragraph 8?

   A noun

   B verb

   C adjective

   D adverb

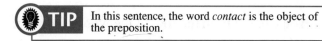 **TIP** In this sentence, the word *contact* is the object of the preposition.

✔ Answers

1 C

Although answer choice A may seem correct, answer choice C is better because dust would make the servant-girl choke.

2 C

The inmates are very rude to the narrator. Answer choice C is the best answer.

3 B

In this instance, the word *walk* means *distance* and therefore is functioning as a noun.

4 B

When the Six Nations desegregated, they were no longer united. Answer choice B is the correct answer.

5 C

You can tell from the root of the word *modernized, modern,* that the correct answer choice is C, *up-to-date*.

6 B

In paragraph 3, the word *advance* is used as a verb.

7 D

Note that in paragraph 10, the writer says that Iroquois art became even more interesting as the world grew more reliant on bland manufactured items. These items are common. Answer choice D is the best answer.

8 B

Annabel Lee was taken away because the angel's envied the love she and the speaker shared. Answer choice B is the best answer.

9 C

The wind chilled Annabel Lee. The word is used as a verb in this sentence.

10 A

The speaker of the poem thinks his soul and Annabel Lee's will always be as one; he says that they will never *dissever*, which means *pull apart or separate*.

11 D

The word *baffling* means *confusing*. Farmers are confused by the crop circles.

12 B

The word *garnered* means *attracted* or *gained*. You can tell this from the context of the word.

13 D

Something that is mundane is boring and common. Answer choice D is the best answer.

14 A

Because the word *contact* is used as the object of the preposition, it is a noun. Answer choice A is the correct answer.

Chapter 2

Vocabulary and Language, Part 2

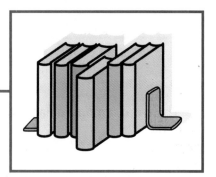

Standard 15: Students will identify and analyze how an author's words appeal to the senses, create imagery, suggest mood, and set tone and provide evidence from the text to support their understanding.

15.7 Evaluate how an author's choice of words advances the theme or purpose of a work.

15.8 Identify and describe the importance of sentence variety in the overall effectiveness of an imaginary/literary or informational/expository work.

Author's Choice of Words

In Chapter 1, you learned how to identify the meanings of unfamiliar vocabulary words—as well as idioms and words with multiple meanings—by using context clues. However, other questions on the MCAS will test your understanding of vocabulary in a different way. These questions will ask you to analyze specific words or phrases in a passage.

When an author writes, he or she chooses words carefully to convey a specific message to readers. An author tries to use words that will appeal to readers' senses to make them taste, hear, see, smell, and feel what he or she is writing about. By using sensory words, an author can create vivid images in the minds of readers. Every deliberate word choice an author makes is meant not only to support the theme of the work but also to communicate his or her purpose for writing. Some of these vocabulary questions will ask you to determine the meaning of a simile, metaphor, or symbol used in a text. Others will ask you to determine why an author uses repetition or varied sentence structure throughout a passage. You might also be asked why the author chose to place emphasis on certain words in a passage—for example, by using **bold**, *italic*, or ALL CAPITAL letters.

Tone and Mood

Other questions on the MCAS will ask you to choose a word that best represents the tone or the mood of the story. The tone reflects the author's attitude about the topic of the passage. If an author is writing about a happy childhood memory, his or her tone might be whimsical or sentimental. If an author is writing a first-person story about a character who is upset, the tone might be angry or sarcastic. The mood of a piece of writing is the feeling the writing evokes in readers. The mood might be mysterious, suspenseful, or reflective. The following table lists words that are commonly used to describe tone and mood.

Common Words Used to Describe Tone and Mood			
ambivalent	encouraging	inspirational	remorseful
amused	enthusiastic	ironic	rude
angry	envious	judgmental	sad
anxious	excited	lighthearted	sarcastic
appreciative	fearful	malicious	sentimental
bewildered	formal	mischievous	serious
bitter	friendly	mysterious	sincere
bored	frustrated	nervous	snobbish
calm	gentle	neutral	suspenseful
cheerful	gloomy	nostalgic	sympathetic
concerned	honest	objective	tense
critical	hopeful	pensive	thankful
curious	humorous	pessimistic	tolerant
defensive	imaginative	proud	tragic
depressed	impersonal	reflective	vindictive
determined	indifferent	relaxed	whimsical
dissatisfied	innocent	relieved	worrisome

Passage 1

Read the following poem. Then answer the questions that follow. Use the Tip below each question to help you choose the correct answer. When you finish, read the answer explanations at the end of this chapter.

The Man He Killed
by Thomas Hardy

"Had he and I but met

By some old ancient inn,

We should have sat us down to wet

Right many a nipperkin![1]

5   "But ranged as infantry,

And staring face to face.

I shot at him and he at me,

And killed him in his place.

"I shot him dead because—

10   Because he was my foe,

Just so; my foe of course he was;

That's clear enough; although

"He thought he'd 'list perhaps,

Off-hand, like—just as I—

15   Was out of work—had sold his traps[2]—

No other reason why.

"Yes, quaint and curious war is!

You shoot a fellow down

You'd treat if met where any bar is,

20   Or help to half-a-crown."

1. *Nipperkin* = cup.

2. *Traps* = personal things.

 Questions

1   What is the effect of the repetition in lines 10 and 11?

A   It emphasizes that the poet and the man were longtime enemies.

B   It indicates that the poet has no regrets about killing the man.

C   It shows that the poet is trying to justify killing the man.

D   It reveals that the man could just as easily have killed the poet.

> **TIP** Read the whole stanza containing lines 10 and 11, paying close attention to how the stanza ends. How does the poet seem to feel about calling the other man a "foe"?

2   What is the effect of using the phrase "quaint and curious" to describe war in line 17?

A   It stresses the danger and uncertainty the poet faced in the war.

B   It expresses the poet's sarcasm and criticism of the war.

C   It demonstrates the poet's fear of fighting in another war.

D   It shows that the poet has remorse over the destruction the war caused.

> **TIP** Look at the words the poet uses to describe war. How are these words different from the words most people would use to describe war? Why do you think the poet chose to describe war this way?

3   Based on the poem, explain how the poet shows that he feels guilty about killing the man. Use relevant and specific information from the poem to support your answer.

_____

> **TIP** Read the poem again and look for clues that express the poet's guilt over killing the man. Consider why the poet killed the man, and how the author would have treated the man under different circumstances.

Passage 2

Read the following poem. Then answer the questions that follow. Use the Tip below each question to help you choose the correct answer. When you finish, read the answer explanations at the end of this chapter.

Ah, Are You Digging on My Grave
by Thomas Hardy

"Ah, are you digging on my grave,

My loved one?—planting rue?"

—"No: yesterday he went to wed

One of the brightest wealth has bred.

5   'It cannot hurt her now,' he said,

'That I should not be true.'"

"Then who is digging on my grave,

My nearest dearest kin?"

—"Ah, no: they sit and think, 'What use!

10   What good will planting flowers produce?

No tendance of her mound can loose

Her spirit from Death's gin.'"

"But someone digs upon my grave?

My enemy?—prodding sly?"

15   —"Nay: when she heard you had passed the Gate

That shuts on all flesh soon or late,

She thought you no more worth her hate,

And cares not where you lie.

"Then, who is digging on my grave?

20   Say—since I have not guessed!"

—"O it is I, my mistress dear,

Your little dog, who still lives near,

And much I hope my movements here

Have not disturbed your rest?"

25   "Ah yes! You dig upon my grave . . .

Why flashed it not to me

That one true heart was left behind!

What feeling do we ever find

To equal among human kind

30   A dog's fidelity!"

"Mistress, I dug upon your grave

To bury a bone, in case

I should be hungry near this spot

When passing on my daily trot.

35   I am sorry, but I quite forgot

It was your resting place."

 Questions

4   In which line does the tone of the poem change dramatically?

A   line 2

B   line 8

C   line 19

D   line 31

> **TIP** Read the poem again. How does the woman in the grave feel when she learns that her dog is digging upon her grave? What is the dog's reason for digging on her grave?

5   In line 15, what does the metaphor "passed the Gate" suggest?

   A   the time at which a person dies

   B   the entrance to the graveyard

   C   the coffin in which the woman is buried

   D   the people the woman left behind

 TIP Read the stanza that contains line 15 again. The dog explains that "the Gate . . . shuts on all flesh soon or late." What does this mean?

6   Which of the following best describes the mood of the poem?

   A   ambivalent

   B   sympathetic

   C   hopeful

   D   whimsical

 TIP Remember, the mood is the feeling the poem evokes in you. How does this poem make you feel?

Passage 3

Read the following passage. Then answer the questions that follow. Use the Tip below each question to help you choose the correct answer. When you finish, read the answer explanations at the end of this chapter.

Lively Lizards

The Colorful Chameleon

1   Standing in the window of the local pet shop, you carefully examine a lizard as it expertly maneuvers along the length of a slim branch, like a tightrope walker at the circus. Having found a comfortable place beneath the warmth of a light bulb, the lizard settles in for a nap. You watch the strange-looking creature for a few more minutes, and just as you are about to walk away, the lizard's bright green skin turns white right before your eyes! Intrigued by the spectacle you have just witnessed, you enter the pet store to learn more about this magnificent magician.

Land of Lizards

2   Wild chameleons live in very few places in the world. Those that are housed as pets in the United States and other places on the continent were shipped from Madagascar, India, Yemen, Kenya, or South Africa. About half of the world's chameleon population, which totals about 135 species, can be found in Madagascar, an island off the coast of Africa. In fact, 59 of the world's chameleon species can only be found in Madagascar, including the largest species, the Parson's chameleon, which can grow to the size of a cat.

Amazing Abilities

3   Chameleons are known for their ability to change the color of their skin. Most people believe that chameleons change color to blend in with their surroundings; however, that is a widespread misconception about these lizards. Chameleons change color according to temperature or mood or to communicate with other chameleons. They do not have an unlimited array of colors, but they can exhibit shades of green, brown, red, blue, yellow, white, or black skin. Despite the fact that many normally appear to be green or brown, the outer layer of a chameleon's skin is actually transparent. It is the layers of skin cells underneath that contain pigments called chromatophores and melanin. These cells expand and contract depending on a chameleon's body temperature or mood. If a chameleon is too warm, its brain will tell the lighter-colored skin cells to enlarge so that it can reflect light off of its body rather than absorbing it. Bright colors are used to attract mates, and dark colors are used to show enemies that the chameleon is ready to attack, if necessary. In self-defense, a chameleon might also hiss and spring at its would-be attacker.

Human Threat

4 A chameleon must avoid snakes and birds because they might eat it, but the greatest threat to the chameleon by far is the human race. When trees are cut down to create farmlands, fuel for heat, or housing materials, the arboreal chameleon has nowhere to live and must seek out a new habitat. Some chameleons adapt well to these changes and successfully discover new dwellings. Others do not fare as well. Agricultural chemicals can also kill off these likable creatures. Another—perhaps greater—threat to chameleon populations is their export for sale in America and other countries. Almost 100,000 chameleons are shipped out of their countries of origin every year. Some are not equipped to survive the transport, and others will not adapt to the North American climate. The ones that do survive the trip are then sold in pet stores and on the Internet. Many countries are working to pass laws banning chameleon export, so that chameleons can live and thrive in their native lands.

⁇ Questions

7 Which of the following best describes the tone of the article?

   A worrisome

   B neutral

   C appreciative

   D enthusiastic

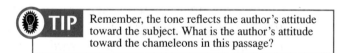

TIP Remember, the tone reflects the author's attitude toward the subject. What is the author's attitude toward the chameleons in this passage?

8   In the article, why is a chameleon changing color to blend in with its surroundings described as a "widespread misconception"?

A   Moving to a new environment is what usually causes chameleons to change the color of their skin.

B   Chameleons have transparent skin and therefore appear to have the same coloring as their surroundings.

C   Chameleons normally change color to distract predators and escape to safety.

D   Temperature, mood, and communication are the main reasons why chameleons change colors.

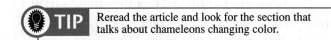

TIP   Reread the article and look for the section that talks about chameleons changing color.

9   What is the effect of the author's use of simile in paragraph 1?

A   It describes for readers how the lizard can change colors.

B   It helps readers visualize a lizard climbing along a small branch.

C   It explains to readers the correct way to create a lizard habitat.

D   It compares the lizard in the window to other lizards in the pet shop.

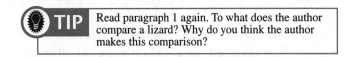

TIP   Read paragraph 1 again. To what does the author compare a lizard? Why do you think the author makes this comparison?

10   What is the author referring to by writing in paragraph 1, "Intrigued by the spectacle you have just witnessed, you enter the pet store to learn more about this magnificent magician"?

A   a pet shop owner with a special talent

B   a magician in the circus

C   a special light that changes colors

D   a lizard in the pet shop

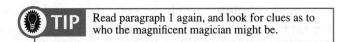

TIP   Read paragraph 1 again, and look for clues as to who the magnificent magician might be.

Passage 4

Read the following passage. Then answer the questions that follow. Use the Tip below each question to help you choose the correct answer. When you finish, read the answer explanations at the end of this chapter.

Excerpt from "The False Gems"
by Guy de Maupassant

1   Monsieur Lantin had met the young girl at a reception at the house of the second head of his department, and had fallen head over heels in love with her. . . . She and her mother came to live in Paris, where the latter, who made the acquaintance of some of the families in her neighborhood, hoped to find a husband for her daughter.

2   They had very moderate means, and were honorable, gentle, and quiet.

3   The young girl was a perfect type of the virtuous woman in whose hands every sensible young man dreams of one day intrusting his happiness. Her simple beauty had the charm of angelic modesty, and the imperceptible smile which constantly hovered about the lips seemed to be the reflection of a pure and lovely soul.

4   Monsieur Lantin . . . enjoyed a snug little salary of three thousand five hundred francs, and he proposed to this model young girl, and was accepted.

5   She governed his household with such clever economy that they seemed to live in luxury. She lavished the most delicate attentions on her husband, coaxed and fondled him; and so great was her charm that six years after their marriage, Monsieur Lantin discovered that he loved his wife even more than during the first days of their honeymoon.

6   He found fault with only two of her tastes: Her love for the theatre, and her taste for imitation jewelry. Her friends (the wives of some petty officials) frequently procured for her a box at the theatre, often for the first representations of the new plays; and her husband was obliged to accompany her, whether he wished it or not, to these entertainments which bored him excessively after his day's work at the office.

7   After a time, Monsieur Lantin begged his wife to request some lady of her acquaintance to accompany her, and to bring her home after the theatre.

8   Now, with her love for the theatre, came also the desire for ornaments. Her costumes remained as before, simple, in good taste, and always modest; but she soon began to adorn her ears with huge rhinestones, which glittered and sparkled like real diamonds.

9   Her husband frequently remonstrated with her, saying:

10   "My dear, as you cannot afford to buy real jewelry, you ought to appear adorned with your beauty and modesty alone, which are the rarest ornaments of your sex." But she would smile sweetly, and say:

11   "What can I do? I am so fond of jewelry. It is my only weakness. We cannot change our nature."

12   Then she would wind the pearl necklace round her fingers, make the facets of the crystal gems sparkle, and say:

13   "Look! are they not lovely? One would swear they were real."

14   . . . Sometimes, of an evening, when they were enjoying a tête-à-tête by the fireside, she would place on the tea table the morocco leather box containing the "trash," as Monsieur Lantin called it. She would examine the false gems with a passionate attention, as though they imparted some deep and secret joy; and she often persisted in passing a necklace around her husband's neck, and, laughing heartily, would exclaim: "How droll you look!" Then she would throw herself into his arms, and kiss him affectionately.

15   One evening, in winter, she had been to the opera, and returned home chilled through and through. The next morning she coughed, and eight days later she died of inflammation of the lungs.

16   Monsieur Lantin's despair was so great that his hair became white in one month. He wept unceasingly; his heart was broken as he remembered her smile, her voice, every charm of his dead wife.

17   Time did not assuage his grief. . . . Everything in his wife's room remained as it was during her lifetime; all her furniture, even her clothing, being left as it was on the day of her death. Here he was wont to seclude himself daily and think of her who had been his treasure—the joy of his existence.

18   But life soon became a struggle. His income, which, in the hands of his wife, covered all household expenses, was now no longer sufficient for his own immediate wants; and he wondered how she could have managed to buy such excellent wine and the rare delicacies which he could no longer procure with his modest resources. . . .

19   One morning, finding himself without a cent in his pocket, he resolved to sell something, and immediately the thought occurred to him of disposing of his wife's paste jewels, for he cherished in his heart a sort of rancor against these "deceptions," which had always irritated him in the past. The very sight of them spoiled, somewhat, the memory of his lost darling.

20   To the last days of her life she had continued to make purchases, bringing home new gems almost every evening, and he turned them over some time before finally deciding to sell

the heavy necklace, which she seemed to prefer, and which, he thought, ought to be worth about six or seven francs; for it was of very fine workmanship, though only imitation.

21   He put it in his pocket, and started out in search of what seemed a reliable jeweler's shop. At length he found one, and went in, feeling a little ashamed to expose his misery, and also to offer such a worthless article for sale. . . .

22   As soon as the proprietor glanced at the necklace, he cried out:

23   "Ah, parbleu! I know it well; it was bought here."

24   Monsieur Lantin, greatly disturbed, asked:

25   "How much is it worth?"

26   "Well, I sold it for twenty thousand francs. I am willing to take it back for eighteen thousand, when you inform me, according to our legal formality, how it came to be in your possession."

27   This time, Monsieur Lantin was dumfounded. He replied:

28   "But—but—examine it well. Until this moment I was under the impression that it was imitation."

29   The jeweler asked:

30   "What is your name, sir?"

31   "Lantin—I am in the employ of the Minister of the Interior. I live at number sixteen Rue des Martyrs."

32   The merchant looked through his books, found the entry, and said: "That necklace was sent to Madame Lantin's address, sixteen Rue des Martyrs, July 20, 1876."

33   The two men looked into each other's eyes—the widower speechless with astonishment; the jeweler scenting a thief. The latter broke the silence.

34   "Will you leave this necklace here for twenty-four hours?" said he; "I will give you a receipt."

35   Monsieur Lantin answered hastily: "Yes, certainly." Then, putting the ticket in his pocket, he left the store. . . .

36   It must have been a present!—a present!—a present, from whom? Why was it given her? . . . A horrible doubt entered his mind—She? Then, all the other jewels must have been presents, too!

37   The sun awoke him next morning, and he began to dress slowly to go to the office. It was hard to work after such shocks. He sent a letter to his employer, requesting to be excused. Then he remembered that he had to return to the jeweler's. . . . It was a lovely day; a clear, blue sky smiled on the busy city below. Men of leisure were strolling about with their hands in their pockets.

38   Monsieur Lantin, observing them, said to himself: "The rich, indeed, are happy. With money it is possible to forget even the deepest sorrow. . . . Oh if I were only rich!" He perceived that he was hungry, but his pocket was empty. He again remembered the necklace. Eighteen thousand francs! Eighteen thousand francs! What a sum!

39   He soon arrived in the Rue de la Paix, opposite the jeweler's. Eighteen thousand francs! Twenty times he resolved to go in, but shame kept him back. He was hungry, however—very hungry—and not a cent in his pocket. He decided quickly, ran across the street, in order not to have time for reflection, and rushed into the store.

40   The proprietor immediately came forward, and politely offered him a chair; the clerks glanced at him knowingly.

41   "I have made inquiries, Monsieur Lantin," said the jeweler, "and if you are still resolved to dispose of the gems, I am ready to pay you the price I offered."

42   "Certainly, sir," stammered Monsieur Lantin.

43   Whereupon the proprietor took from a drawer eighteen large bills, counted, and handed them to Monsieur Lantin, who signed a receipt; and, with trembling hand, put the money into his pocket.

45   As he was about to leave the store, he turned toward the merchant, who still wore the same knowing smile, and lowering his eyes, said:

46   "I have—I have other gems, which came from the same source. Will you buy them, also?"

47   The merchant bowed: "Certainly, sir."

48   …An hour later, he returned with the gems . . . making the sum of one hundred and forty-three thousand francs.

49   The jeweler remarked, jokingly:

50   "There was a person who invested all her savings in precious stones."

51   Monsieur Lantin replied, seriously:

52   "It is only another way of investing one's money."

53   That day he lunched at Voisin's, and drank wine worth twenty francs a bottle. Then he hired a carriage and made a tour of the Bois. He gazed at the various turnouts with a kind of disdain, and could hardly refrain from crying out to the occupants:

54   "I, too, am rich!—I am worth two hundred thousand francs."

55   For the first time in his life, he was not bored at the theatre, and spent the remainder of the night in a gay frolic.

56   Six months afterward, he married again. His second wife was a very virtuous woman; but had a violent temper. She caused him much sorrow.

⑦ Questions

11   In paragraph 1, what does the phrase "head over heels" mean?

   A   Monsieur Lantin was uncoordinated.

   B   Monsieur Lantin made very little money.

   C   Monsieur Lantin cared deeply for his wife.

   D   Monsieur Lantin was a very intelligent man.

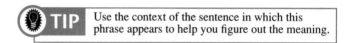

TIP Use the context of the sentence in which this phrase appears to help you figure out the meaning.

12   Read these sentences from paragraph 36 in the story.

> It must have been a present!—a present!—a present, from whom? Why was it given her? . . . A horrible doubt entered his mind—She?

What does Monsieur Lantin mean in these lines?

   A   He thinks that his wife was receiving gifts from another man.

   B   He believes that his wife spent too much money on the gems.

   C   He is afraid that his wife stole the gems from the jewelry store.

   D   He is afraid that his wife had more money than he knew about.

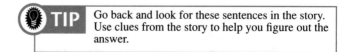

TIP Go back and look for these sentences in the story. Use clues from the story to help you figure out the answer.

13 Based on the story, explain how the author's choice of words foreshadows that Monsieur Lantin's wife's jewels are real. Use relevant and specific information from the article to support your answer.

_____

 TIP Look for instances in the story in which the author stresses that the jewels are imitations. How does this help to foreshadow that they are in fact real jewels?

14 Which word best describes Monsieur Lantin's tone in paragraph 28?

   A remorseful

   B bewildered

   C defensive

   D sarcastic

 TIP Read paragraph 28 again. Why does Monsieur Lantin react to the owner of the jewelry store the way he does?

✔ Answers

1 **C**

The poet does not seem convinced that the man was a "foe," so he keeps repeating the word to try to justify the killing.

2 **B**

The poet uses the words "quaint and curious" to be sarcastic because he does not approve of war and feels guilty that he had to kill a man during a war.

3 **Sample answer**

The poet expresses his guilt over killing the man in several ways. First, he explains that had he and the man met "at some old ancient inn," they probably would have become friends, but because they met on the battlefield, he considered the man a foe and killed him. In the third stanza, he repeats the word "foe," which makes it seem as though he is trying to convince himself that the man was really an enemy and to justify the killing. However, at the end of the poem, he refers to war as "quaint and curious," which seems like a sarcastic way of showing that he is critical of war and feels guilty that he had to kill a man whom he otherwise would have considered a friend.

4 **D**

Throughout the poem, the woman in the grave is curious about who is digging on her grave and is then thrilled to learn that it is her faithful little dog. However, in the last stanza, the tone turns gloomy and bitter when we learn that the dog is just looking for a good place to hide a treat.

5 **A**

The woman in the poem is speaking from her grave, so it can be assumed that when the dog says that she "passed the Gate," it is referring to the time at which she passed away.

6 **B**

The mood in this poem is sympathetic. The poet wants readers to feel bad for the woman in the grave because she seems to have been forgotten by everyone, including her little dog.

7 **B**

The tone of this article is neutral. The author is simply giving information about chameleons. He or she does not seem worried, appreciative, or enthusiastic about the topic.

8   D

According to the article, chameleons do not change color to blend in with their surroundings; rather, they change color to regulate body temperature, express mood changes, and communicate.

9   B

The author compares the lizard walking on the branch to a tightrope walker at the circus. This comparison helps readers picture the lizard as it teeters on a thin branch in the window of the pet shop.

10   D

In this sentence, the author is referring to the lizard in the pet shop. The lizard is likened to a "magnificent magician" because it has changed colors.

11   C

According to the passage, Monsieur Lantin fell "head over heels" in love with his wife. This is an expression that means he deeply cared about her.

12   A

The owner of the jewelry store told Monsieur Lantin that the gems were sent to his address, which means they were not stolen. Therefore, Monsieur Lantin thinks that his wife must have been getting the gems as presents from someone else, possibly another man.

13   Sample answer

The author drops several clues throughout the story to foreshadow that the jewels are real. For example, in paragraph 13, Monsieur Lantin's wife wraps the jewels around her finger and remarks, "One would swear they were real." Later, the author writes, "She would examine the false gems with a passionate attention, as though they imparted some deep and secret joy." This line suggests that Lantin's wife knows something about the gems that she has not shared with her husband.

14   B

Until he arrives at the jewelry store, Monsieur Lantin thinks the jewels are imitations. When the owner offers him a lot of money for them, he has a hard time understanding that they are real.

Chapter 3

Main Idea and Supporting Details

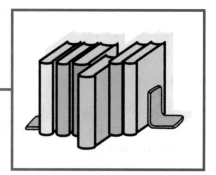

Standard 8: Students will identify the basic facts and main ideas in a text and use them as the basis for interpretation.

Fiction

8.29 Identify and analyze patterns of imagery or symbolism.

8.30 Identify and interpret themes and give supporting evidence from a text.

Nonfiction

8.31 Analyze the logic and use of evidence in an author's argument.

Main Idea

The main idea of a passage is what it is mostly about. You will be asked to identify the main ideas of passages on the MCAS. For many of these questions, the answers are not directly stated in the texts. You will have to read the passages carefully and determine what they are mostly about or determine the most important points. Be aware, however, that in a nonfiction passage, the main idea or thesis is often given in the introduction. Sometimes the title also offers a clue. If the main idea is not stated in the passage, as in fictional passages, ask yourself what the story or poem is mostly about. Choose the answer option that tells what the entire passage—not just part of the passage—is about.

Some questions will ask you to identify the main idea of only part of the passage. For these questions, you might be given several lines of a passage and asked to determine the message the author is implying. For fictional passages, you might also be asked what idea is most important to a character at a particular time.

Supporting Details

A passage will also contain supporting details, which are points that support the main idea or theme. For most questions on supporting details, you will be able to look back at the passage to find the correct answer.

Passage 1

Read the following passage. Then answer the questions that follow. Use the Tip below each question to help you choose the correct answer. When you finish, read the answer explanations at the end of this chapter.

Ripe Figs
by Kate Chopin

1 Maman-Nainaine said that when the figs were ripe Babette might go to visit her cousins down on Bayou-Boeuf, where the sugar cane grows. Not that the ripening of figs had the least thing to do with it, but that is the way Maman-Nainaine was.

2 It seemed to Babette a very long time to wait; for the leaves upon the trees were tender yet, and the figs were like little hard, green marbles.

3 But warm rains came along and plenty of strong sunshine; and though Maman-Nainaine was as patient as the statue of la Madone, and Babette as restless as a humming-bird, the first thing they both knew it was hot summer-time. Every day Babette danced out to where the fig-trees were in a long line against the fence. She walked slowly beneath them, carefully peering between the gnarled, spreading branches. But each time she came disconsolate away again. What she saw there finally was something that made her sing and dance the whole day long.

4 When Maman-Nainaine sat down in her stately way to breakfast, the following morning, her muslin cap standing like an aureole about her white, placid face, Babette approached. She bore a dainty porcelain platter, which she set down before her godmother. It contained a dozen purple figs, fringed around with their rich, green leaves.

5 "Ah," said Maman-Nainaine, arching her eyebrows, "how early the figs have ripened this year!"

6 "Oh," said Babette, "I think they have ripened very late."

7 "Babette," continued Maman-Nainaine, as she peeled the very plumpest figs with her pointed silver fruit-knife, "you will carry my love to them all down on Bayou-Boeuf. And tell your tante Frosine I shall look for her at Toussaint—when the chrysanthemums are in bloom."

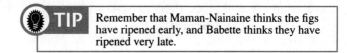 Questions

1 According to the passage, what is the **most** important lesson Maman-Nainaine wants to teach Babette?

　A　You will appreciate things more if you wait for them.

　B　Figs take a long time to ripen.

　C　Looking forward to something special is great fun.

　D　It is important to learn to be patient.

> **TIP** Remember that Maman-Nainaine thinks the figs have ripened early, and Babette thinks they have ripened very late.

2 Which sentence **best** states the main idea of the passage?

　A　The young and the old view time differently.

　B　Some people are more patient than others.

　C　Planning an important trip takes time.

　D　Waiting for figs to ripen can be frustrating.

> **TIP** Consider what the entire story is about. Maman-Nainaine and Babette are very different.

3 According to the passage, when does Maman-Nainaine say she will go to Toussaint?

　A　during the heat of summer

　B　when the sugar cane grows

　C　when the chrysanthemums bloom

　D　when the figs have ripened

> **TIP** This question asks about a supporting detail. Reread the end of the story if you are unsure of the answer.

Passage 2

Read the following passage. Then answer the questions that follow. Use the Tip below each question to help you choose the correct answer. When you finish, read the answer explanations at the end of this chapter.

The Coolest Invention

1 It often gets very hot during the summer. Long ago, few people could even bear to live in the southern United States because of the high temperatures. Many kinds of technology have been created since then to make hot climates more comfortable. Primary among these tools is the air conditioner.

2 We may take air conditioners for granted today, but they are very important to many aspects of modern life. Air conditioners not only make our houses cool but also help factories and businesses run efficiently year-round. They keep food, drinks, and medicines fresh and safe. They even protect paper from shrinking and film and paintings from warping.

3 People have tried to build cooling machines for well over a hundred years. The earliest air conditioners were giant pumps that sent dangerous chemicals through pipes. This did cause some cooling, but the toxic, flammable chemicals also caused poisoning and fires.

4   The first safe, modern air conditioner was invented by Willis Haviland Carrier in 1902. Just a year after completing his studies as an engineer, Carrier had a "flash of genius." While waiting for a train, he watched the fog and thought about humidity and temperature. By the time the train arrived, Carrier had figured out a formula that would allow a machine to control the temperature.

5   That same year, Carrier was hired to solve a big problem for a book publisher. The heat and humidity in the printing factory caused the paper to swell. The printers found it difficult to add different-colored inks to the pages because the pages kept warping. Carrier put his "flash of genius" to work and built the first air conditioner. Once installed in the factory, the air conditioner kept the temperature stable. The paper no longer warped. The publishers were thrilled with the device, and Carrier knew he had something special.

6   In 1906, Carrier revealed his perfected machine. The term *air conditioner* did not catch on until later. At the time, Carrier called his invention the Apparatus for Treating Air. Many industries purchased Carrier's machines, and in 1915, he went into business.

7   Carrier kept on improving his machines for use in factories and businesses. He did not start thinking about keeping people cool until 1924, when he was asked to install his machines in a department store. Then he installed some in movie theaters. People loved the technology and swarmed to businesses that featured the air-cooling devices.

8   The next great challenge for Carrier was creating an air conditioner that people could use in their homes. In 1928, he designed the Weathermaker, a small, safe household unit. Over the following decades, thousands of people purchased Carrier's machines. Today, air-conditioning is a staple in many homes and businesses—all thanks to Willis Haviland Carrier.

(?) Questions

4   According to the article, what made Carrier invent the first air conditioner? Use information and details from the article to support your answer.

_____

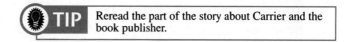

TIP Reread the part of the story about Carrier and the book publisher.

5   According to the article, what was a problem with the first cooling machines?

A   They created a fog.

B   They heated too quickly.

C   They were extremely loud.

D   They used toxic chemicals.

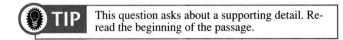

TIP This question asks about a supporting detail. Re-read the beginning of the passage.

6   What is this article **mainly** about?

A   why a man invented the first air conditioner

B   why air conditioners are used to cool factories

C   what the first air conditioner was like

D   the life of an inventor named Willis Carrier

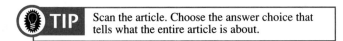

TIP Scan the article. Choose the answer choice that tells what the entire article is about.

Passage 3

Read the following passage. Then answer the questions that follow. Use the Tip below each question to help you choose the correct answer. When you finish, read the answer explanations at the end of this chapter.

The Thinking Spot

1   It was a Saturday afternoon, and I was supposed to be writing a journal entry for Monday's English class about my fondest childhood memory. Unfortunately, the rhythmic blinking of the cursor was the only movement on my otherwise blank computer screen. Frustrated, I let my eyes wander to the window. The mammoth oak tree in my backyard dominated most of the view. Fresh leaves the vivid green of spring fluttered in the breeze and the old swing that hung from the tree's largest branch gently swayed back and forth. "My thinking spot," I said aloud. Leaving all thoughts of homework assignments behind, I went outside.

2   I circled the old swing several times, tugging the ropes to make sure they weren't rotted and rubbing my hand across the wooden seat to check for splinters. Deeming it safe for use, I hoisted myself onto the seat and pumped my legs back and forth. Though it had probably been six or seven years since my last outing on the swing, the pendulum-like motion felt familiar and comfortable. I remembered why this had once been my favorite place to sit and contemplate the world. As the swing traveled back and forth, my mind opened and thoughts deluged my brain.

3   Suddenly, I was five years old again, begging my grandpa to push me on the swing. "C'mon, Gramp," I would plead, adding the one phrase I knew he couldn't resist: "Pretty please with a cherry on top." Whether it was the missing front tooth in my awkward smile or the unraveling braids of my brown hair, Gramp would grin and crumble and I would have my way. Within minutes, we would traipse hand-in-hand across the dew-covered lawn toward the swing.

4   "Hold on tight," he would say, as he gave the swing a hefty push to get it started. I would smile and giggle as the swing flew higher and higher into the air. Soon I could see over the Millers' fence, right into their pool, and catch a glimpse of the football stuck in the Carmichaels' gutter. I could see the patch of shingles on the roof of my house where Dad had patched a leak during a rainstorm. Wispy strands of hair would fly away from my face and then tickle my cheeks and forehead as the swing moved forward and backward.

5   As darkness fell, Gramp would slow the swing to a stop and lift me onto his shoulders. We would return to the house, following the dim glow cast from the kitchen window. Once inside, Gramp would settle into an armchair, I would climb onto his lap, and he would read me a book of children's poems by Robert Louis Stevenson. When he reached my favorite rhyme, I would recite it right along with him: "Oh how I love to go up in a swing."

6   When Gramp wasn't around, sometimes I could convince my older brother, George, to push me on the swing. George's technique was much different than Gramp's. Instead of starting out slow and allowing the swing to steadily fly higher and higher, George would pull the swing as far back and as high as he could—sometimes I felt as if I might slip right out of the seat!—and then he would run, full speed, right underneath the swing. "Underdog!" he would yell as he released the ropes, and I would shriek with a combination of excited delight and fear that I would swing upside-down, right over the tree branch.

7   By the time I was nine years old, Gramp had moved into a nursing home and George had gotten his driver's license and wasn't home much. It was up to me to get my swing moving faster and higher, and to create my own thrilling adventures. In my mind, my swing had been my spaceship, rocketing around the universe at record speeds, and my Pegasus, the flying horse of Greek mythology. It had been my trapeze, my time machine, and the dragon I had tamed as the world's fiercest female knight. But most of all, my swing had been my "thinking spot," the one place where I knew I could completely lose myself in thought. Riding my swing, I must have composed thousands of songs and poems, and hundreds of scenarios for my friends and me to act out.

8   That Saturday on the swing was no different. As I scuffed my feet through the worn patch of grass beneath the swing and gradually came to a stop, I felt as though I had accomplished the impossible. Returning to my computer, my fingers danced across the keyboard and I watched as the screen filled with the fondest memory from my childhood: my thinking spot.

(?) Questions

7   According to the story, what did the narrator do when her grandfather finished pushing her on the swing?

A   write about the experience in a journal

B   go in the house and look for George

C   create her own thrilling adventures

D   listen to her grandfather read poetry

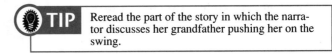 **TIP** Reread the part of the story in which the narrator discusses her grandfather pushing her on the swing.

8   Describe what the narrator remembers about the way her brother George pushed her on the swing. Use relevant and specific information from the story to support your answer.

_____

 Reread paragraph 6 of the story.

9   Read this sentence from paragraph 7 in the passage.

> It had been my trapeze, my time machine, and the dragon I had tamed as the world's fiercest female knight.

What is the narrator implying?

A   She learned how to do many different activities on the swing.

B   The swing has been in her yard as long as she can remember.

C   Swinging on the swing helped cultivate her imagination.

D   A good way to clear your mind is to swing on a swing.

 Reread paragraph 7 and look for clues as to what the author might mean.

10   What is this story **mainly** about?

A   remembering special times shared with a grandfather

B   struggling to write a journal entry for English class

C   taking comfort in fond memories of swinging on a swing

D   enjoying swinging on a swing even as an adult

 To answer this question correctly, you need to determine what most of the story is about. You need to choose the main idea, not a supporting detail.

Passage 4

Read the following passage. Then answer the questions that follow. Use the Tip below each question to help you choose the correct answer. When you finish, read the answer explanations at the end of this chapter.

Excerpt from *Hamlet*
by William Shakespeare

Hamlet's father, the King of Denmark, has recently died. Shortly after the king's death, Hamlet's mother married Hamlet's uncle, Claudius, who is now the new king. After hearing from his friends that a ghost resembling his father has been sighted wandering around the castle, Hamlet has agreed to stand watch with them at the castle gates in hopes of seeing his father's figure appear.

Scene IV. The platform.

[*Enter Hamlet, Horatio, and Marcellus.*]

HAMLET: The air bites shrewdly; it is very cold.

HORATIO: It is a nipping and an eager air.

5   HAMLET: What hour now?

HORATIO: I think it lacks of twelve.

MARCELLUS: No, it is struck.

HORATIO: Indeed? I heard it not: then draws near the season

Wherein the spirit held his wont to walk. . . .

10   Look, my lord, it comes!

[*Enter GHOST:*]

HAMLET: Angels and ministers of grace defend us!—

Be thou a spirit of health or goblin damn'd,

Bring with thee airs from heaven or blasts from hell,

15   Be thy intents wicked or charitable,

Thou com'st in such a questionable shape

That I will speak to thee: I'll call thee Hamlet,

King, father, royal Dane; O, answer me!

Let me not burst in ignorance; but tell

20 Why thy canoniz'd bones, hearsed in death,

Have burst their cerements; why the sepulchre,

Wherein we saw thee quietly in-urn'd,

Hath op'd his ponderous and marble jaws

To cast thee up again! What may this mean,

25 That thou, dead corse, again in complete steel,

Revisit'st thus the glimpses of the moon,

Making night hideous, and we fools of nature

So horridly to shake our disposition

With thoughts beyond the reaches of our souls?

30 Say, why is this? wherefore? what should we do?

[*Ghost beckons Hamlet.*]

HORATIO: It beckons you to go away with it,

As if it some impartment did desire

To you alone.

35 MARCELLUS: Look with what courteous action

It waves you to a more removed ground:

But do not go with it!

HORATIO: No, by no means.

HAMLET: It will not speak; then will I follow it.

40 HORATIO: Do not, my lord.

HAMLET: Why, what should be the fear?

I do not set my life at a pin's fee;

And for my soul, what can it do to that,

Being a thing immortal as itself?

45 It waves me forth again;—I'll follow it.

HORATIO: What if it tempt you toward the flood, my lord,

Or to the dreadful summit of the cliff

That beetles o'er his base into the sea,

And there assume some other horrible form

50   Which might deprive your sovereignty of reason,

And draw you into madness? think of it:

The very place puts toys of desperation,

Without more motive, into every brain

That looks so many fadoms to the sea

55   And hears it roar beneath.

HAMLET: It waves me still.—

Go on; I'll follow thee.

MARCELLUS: You shall not go, my lord.

HAMLET: Hold off your hands.

60   HORATIO: Be rul'd; you shall not go.

HAMLET: My fate cries out,

And makes each petty artery in this body

As hardy as the Nemean lion's nerve.—

[*Ghost beckons.*]

65   Still am I call'd;—unhand me, gentlemen;—

[*Breaking free from them.*]

By heaven, I'll make a ghost of him that lets me!—

I say, away!—Go on; I'll follow thee.

[*Exeunt Ghost and Hamlet.*]

70   HORATIO: He waxes desperate with imagination.

MARCELLUS: Let's follow; 'tis not fit thus to obey him.

HORATIO: Have after.—To what issue will this come?

MARCELLUS: Something is rotten in the state of Denmark.

HORATIO: Heaven will direct it.

75   MARCELLUS: Nay, let's follow him.

   [*Exeunt.*]

Scene V. A more remote part of the Castle.

[*Enter Ghost and Hamlet.*]

HAMLET: Whither wilt thou lead me? speak! I'll go no further.

80   GHOST: Mark me.

HAMLET: I will.

GHOST: My hour is almost come,

When I to sulph'uous and tormenting flames

Must render up myself.

85   HAMLET: Alas, poor ghost!

GHOST: Pity me not, but lend thy serious hearing

To what I shall unfold.

HAMLET: Speak; I am bound to hear.

GHOST: So art thou to revenge, when thou shalt hear.

90   HAMLET: What?

GHOST: I am thy father's spirit;

Doom'd for a certain term to walk the night,

And for the day confin'd to waste in fires,

Till the foul crimes done in my days of nature

95   Are burnt and purg'd away. But that I am forbid

To tell the secrets of my prison-house,

I could a tale unfold whose lightest word

Would harrow up thy soul; freeze thy young blood;

Make thy two eyes, like stars, start from their spheres;

100   Thy knotted and combined locks to part,

And each particular hair to stand on end

Like quills upon the fretful porcupine:

But this eternal blazon must not be

To ears of flesh and blood.—List, list, O, list!—

105   If thou didst ever thy dear father love— . . .

Revenge his foul and most unnatural murder.

HAMLET: Murder!

GHOST: Murder most foul, as in the best it is;

But this most foul, strange, and unnatural.

110   HAMLET: Haste me to know't, that I, with wings as swift

As meditation or the thoughts of love,

May sweep to my revenge.

GHOST: I find thee apt;

And duller shouldst thou be than the fat weed

115   That rots itself in ease on Lethe wharf,

Wouldst thou not stir in this. Now, Hamlet, hear.

'Tis given out that, sleeping in my orchard,

A serpent stung me; so the whole ear of Denmark

Is by a forged process of my death

120   Rankly abus'd; but know, thou noble youth,

The serpent that did sting thy father's life

Now wears his crown.

HAMLET: O my prophetic soul!

Mine uncle!

⦾ Questions

11 According to the excerpt, why does the ghost want to talk to Hamlet?

  A He wants to tell him not to pity him.

  B He wants to keep him from the flames.

  C He wants to warn him of the future.

  D He wants to tell him how he died.

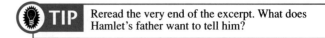 **TIP**   Reread the very end of the excerpt. What does Hamlet's father want to tell him?

12 According to the excerpt, why are Horatio and Marcellus hesitant to let Hamlet go with the ghost?

A They fear the ghost will hurt him.

B They worry Claudius will find out.

C They think the ghost is a trick.

D They fear he will never return.

TIP | Reread the conversation between Horatio and Hamlet.

13 According to the excerpt, why can't the ghost tell Hamlet what happens at the prison-house?

A He would burn in the flames.

B He is forbidden to discuss it.

C Hamlet would seek revenge.

D Others might overhear.

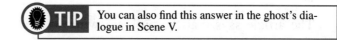

TIP | You can also find this answer in the ghost's dialogue in Scene V.

14 According to the excerpt, what actually caused the death of Hamlet's father?

A He was killed by Hamlet's uncle.

B He was bitten by a poisonous snake.

C He passed away in his sleep.

D He got trapped in a raging fire.

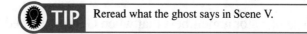

TIP | Reread what the ghost says in Scene V.

✔ Answers

1 D

The reason Maman-Nainaine makes Babette wait until the figs ripen is to teach her patience. Answer choice D is the correct answer.

2 A

The story implies that patience is something that is learned with age. Waiting is harder for the young. Answer choice A is the best answer.

3 C

The answer to this question is at the end of the story. Maman-Nainaine says she will go to Toussaint when the chrysanthemums are in bloom.

4 Sample answer

Carrier first created an air conditioner when he was hired to solve a big problem for a book publisher: the heat and humidity in the printing factory made the paper swell and the pages warp. Carrier created an air conditioner to solve this problem.

5 D

The article says that the problem with the first cooling machine was that it used toxic chemicals that sometimes caused fires.

6 A

The article discusses how and why Carrier came up with the idea for the first air conditioner and how he improved on air conditioners over time.

7 D

The narrator explains that when she finished swinging, she and her grandfather would go into the house and read children's poems together.

8 Sample answer

The narrator remembers that when George pushed her on the swing, it seemed more exciting because he would push her up as high as he could and then let go. She mentions that she sometimes felt as though she would swing right over the tree branch because she went so high. The narrator thought the way George pushed her on the swing was thrilling.

9 C

The narrator writes that while she was on the swing, she often thought up stories and songs and imagined that her swing was many different things. Answer choice C is correct.

10 C

Answer choices A, B, and D are details from the story. The whole passage is about the narrator's pleasant memories of swinging on the swing.

11 D

Although the ghost does tell Hamlet not to pity him, he has come to tell Hamlet that his uncle is a murderous traitor.

12 A

Horatio warns Hamlet that the ghost may tempt him toward a flood or the dreadful summit of the cliff. He and Marcellus fear the ghost will harm Hamlet.

13 B

According to lines 95 and 96, the ghost is "forbid to tell the secrets" of the prison-house. Answer choice B is correct.

14 A

In lines 117 through 122, the ghost of Hamlet's father explains that the people of Denmark were told that he was bitten by a snake. However, he tells Hamlet that the "snake" wears his crown, revealing that he was actually murdered by Claudius, Hamlet's uncle.

Chapter 4
Short Stories

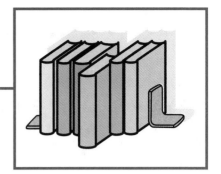

Standard 11: Students will identify, analyze, and apply knowledge of theme in a literary work and provide evidence from the text to support their understanding.

    11.5 Apply knowledge of the concept that the theme or meaning of a selection represents a view or comment on life, and provide support from the text for the identified theme.

Standard 12: Students will identify, analyze, and apply knowledge of the structure and elements of fiction and provide evidence from the text to support their understanding.

    12.5 Locate and analyze such elements in fiction as point of view, foreshadowing, and irony.

Elements of Fiction

Questions on the MCAS for these standards will be on fiction passages. These questions ask about literary elements, such as character, plot, and theme. They may be multiple-choice or open-response questions.

Some questions will address characterization—how the character acts or thinks and how those actions and thoughts affect the plot of the story. These questions might ask you why a character does a certain thing or how he or she feels about something.

Most short stories contain a conflict, which is a major problem that the characters must face. Some questions on the MCAS will ask you to identify the conflict. Others might ask you how a character resolves the conflict. This is called the resolution.

Questions for these standards will also be about theme or plot. Often you will be asked to compare parts of a story and find a theme, which is the idea that recurs throughout the passage and provides a view or comment on life. Questions might ask how an author's choices, such as point of view, affect how the plot is revealed to readers.

Other questions might ask you about literary terms, like *irony*, which is a way of stating something that means the opposite of the literal meaning. You might also be asked about foreshadowing, a hint of what will happen later in the story.

Finally, questions on the MCAS might ask you to support your answers with evidence from the text. When a question asks you to support your answer with evidence, you will need to provide examples from the passage.

Passage 1

Read the following passage. Then answer the questions that follow. Use the Tip below each question to help you choose the correct answer. When you finish, read the answer explanations at the end of this chapter.

A Superstition Mission

1 "The exam will be on Monday," announced Mrs. Keenan, the science teacher. "You'll have the entire weekend, so there will be *no excuse* for forgetting to prepare!"

2 Pete squirmed in his seat, his mind racing with considerations of all of the tasks he'd need to perform before the exam. The exam would cover the first five chapters in their massive textbook—chapters that covered topics ranging from earth science to space exploration. He found the material difficult and knew he'd have to really make an effort to get a decent grade.

3 Mentally reviewing his schedule for the weekend, Pete knew right away he'd need to dedicate most of his time over the next few days to preparing for Mrs. Keenan's test. He was going to start preparing immediately after school, but he remembered that it was Friday the thirteenth. Not wanting to jinx himself, Pete instead resolved to start preparing bright and early on Saturday morning. On Friday night, he placed his textbook at the head of his bed and stacked next to it a pile of science handout sheets.

4 "Here's everything I need to absorb by Monday afternoon," he thought, plopping a pillow on top of it all. "So I'll start by sleeping on it so maybe the information will soak up into my brain."

5 Pete rested his tired head on the pillow. Though the pillow was lumpy from all the papers underneath, Pete knew his discomfort was necessary. He didn't want a single thing to go wrong with his preparation routine.

6 Pete woke up at nine o'clock on Saturday, since nine was his lucky number. He'd spent the night dreaming, wading in the deluge of science topics he needed to master by Monday. He realized now more than ever that he needed some special preparations. For breakfast he ate some cereal with marshmallows shaped like traditional good-luck charms, like horseshoes and four-leaf clovers. "This'll fill me up with good luck," he thought as he scanned through the topics of his textbook.

7   Each time he saw a new chapter heading in his book, he thought of an appropriate activity to help him absorb its information. For the chapter on the revolutions of planets, he spun his textbook around three times—three was another lucky number for him. Then he spun his chair around, too, for good measure. When he saw information about the winds that blew across Earth, he remembered a good-luck ritual of blowing on his hands.

8   "Maybe that'll help my hands write down the correct answers on Monday," Pete thought hopefully.

9   Again, he slept with the textbook and handouts under his pillow, and all day Sunday he observed every superstitious ritual he could think of. He didn't step on any cracks in the sidewalk, he entered and exited his house through the same door, and he kept well away from any roving black cats. Then, on Sunday night, Pete carefully chose his lucky sweatshirt, his lucky socks, and his lucky baseball cap. He even accessorized with a lucky charm that his grandmother had given him years ago.

10   Pete was feeling confident as he swaggered into class, assured that his weekend of preparation would pay off. Mrs. Keenan passed out the exams and Pete grabbed his enthusiastically, gripping his old, chewed-up lucky pencil.

11   The next day, Pete found out that he'd failed the test. He shook his head in amazement. "I did everything I could to prepare," he said. "Who'd have thought I'd forget to read the book?"

(?) Questions

1   In the excerpt, Pete spends **most** of his time doing which of the following?

   A   studying for the test

   B   worrying about the test

   C   trying to create luck

   D   talking to his friends

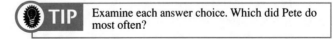
TIP Examine each answer choice. Which did Pete do most often?

2   In paragraph 1, why are the words *no excuse* italicized?

   A   to emphasize Mrs. Keenan's warning

   B   to emphasize Mrs. Keenan's anger

   C   to emphasize Mrs. Keenan's meanness

   D   to emphasize Mrs. Keenan's surprise

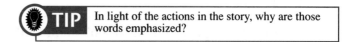

TIP In light of the actions in the story, why are those words emphasized?

3   According to the excerpt, which of the following would **best** describe Pete?

   A   lazy

   B   annoyed

   C   clever

   D   foolish

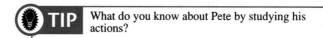

TIP What do you know about Pete by studying his actions?

Passage 2

Read the following passage. Then answer the questions that follow. Use the Tip below each question to help you choose the correct answer. When you finish, read the answer explanations at the end of this chapter.

Logan's Lesson

1 Logan slammed the passenger door of his father's pickup truck and gazed warily at the main entrance of the Oceanside Nursing Home. He groaned inwardly and trudged toward the door, each step feeling heavier than the previous one.

2 Inside, Logan was greeted by a receptionist with a smile the size of all of New England and more perkiness in her greeting than Logan had been able to muster in his entire life. Her name tag said Suzanne. "You must be Logan," she chirped. "I can't *wait* for you to meet our residents."

3 Suzanne motioned for Logan to follow her, and he struggled to maintain the Olympic pace she set as she sped down a long corridor toward a set of double doors. A sign near the doors indicated that he was standing outside the Recreation Room. Peering through the window, Logan spied about a dozen silver-haired men and women in the room. Two men played a game of checkers in the corner, while another maneuvered a small scooter toward a rack of magazines. A few women sat in a circle of rocking chairs around a television watching a news program. One of them held yarn and knitting needles in her lap. On the far side of the room, one elderly man with white hair sat at a table by himself carving something from a small scrap of wood.

4 "That's Hector. I think you two will get along quite nicely," said Suzanne, pointing to the man at the far table.

5 Suzanne's pager began to beep, and after glancing at the numbers, she sprinted down the corridor. "I'm afraid you're on your own, Logan. I've got to get back to the reception area," she explained as she disappeared around the corner.

6 Logan sighed, shifted his backpack to his left shoulder, and shuffled toward Hector's table. As Logan extended his hand to introduce himself, Hector spoke. "Troublemaker, eh?"

7 Logan stepped back and withdrew his hand, the puzzled look on his face prompting Hector to continue.

8 "They always send me the troublemakers," he said, turning back to his wooden sculpture. "That, and your black eye gave you away."

9   Logan raised his hand to touch the painful bruise near his right eye. Hector's insights were correct. Logan's punishment for getting into a fight at school was to spend at least one hour every day at the nursing home until the end of the semester. Mr. Weatherby, the principal at Logan's high school, thought that spending time with some of the elderly residents at Oceanside would help him learn to care about others' thoughts and feelings.

10   Logan settled into the chair across from Hector. He watched silently as sawdust and shavings fell from the scrap of wood in Hector's wrinkled hands, until finally, Hector set down his carving knife and placed the finished sculpture on the table. Logan carefully examined the petite form, amazed by the intricate details etched into the wood. It was a boxer wearing a helmet and boxing gloves, his feet slightly separated and his arms in a position indicating that he was ready to fight.

11   Logan glanced at Hector. "A fighter for a fighter," said the old man. With that, he lifted himself from his chair and moved toward the door.

12   "Wait," said Logan. "Aren't we supposed to talk or something?"

13   Hector turned around and winked, then disappeared through the double doors. Glancing at his watch, Logan realized that an hour had already passed and that his father would be waiting for him. He scooped the wooden figurine off the table, wrapped it in a tissue, and placed it in the zippered pouch of his backpack.

14   Logan remained quiet on the way home, thinking about the unusual events of the afternoon. Hector had called him a troublemaker and a fighter. It was a fitting description, but Logan had never intended to be either. It just seemed that sometimes, when someone or something made him angry or upset, he felt the need to release his anger, and the easiest way to do that was to punch, kick, or break something.

15   That night, Logan rummaged through his backpack until he found the boxer statue. Placing it on his desk, he stared at it for a long time. When he finally crawled into bed, he knew what he could discuss with Hector.

16   The next day, Logan looked for Hector in the Recreation Room, but he was nowhere to be found. Returning to the reception area, Logan ask Suzanne for directions to Hector's living quarters, but she informed him that Hector was on the balcony outside the craft room on the second floor. At the top of the steps, Logan made a left as Suzanne had instructed and walked the length of a blue hallway. He opened a door on the left and entered a room lined with shelves and overflowing with cans of paint, bottles of glue, stacks of paper, and a mishmash of other art supplies. Through the sliding door, Logan could see Hector standing at an easel, and beyond him, a magnificent view of the Atlantic Ocean.

17   "You paint, too," said Logan as he stepped outside.

18   Hector turned toward Logan, revealing a painting so similar to the ocean view Logan had just admired that the boy wondered if he was looking through an empty frame.

19   "What else do you do?" Logan asked.

20   Hector thought for a moment and then explained that his numerous creative activities corresponded to how he felt at a particular point in time. When feeling happy or peaceful, he painted, and when feeling lonely or sad, he wrote poetry. When nervous, such as when he's about to meet someone new, he liked to whittle away at a piece of wood. Logan smiled, thinking of the wooden boxer. He was amazed by Hector's artistic abilities—poetry, paintings, drawings, sculptures, and carvings—each chosen to convey a certain mood, thought, or feeling.

21   "What do you do when you're angry?" asked Logan.

22   This time it was Hector who smiled. "I build things. Whether it's a chair, a table, or a simple puzzle, building things helps me release my anger *con*structively, rather than *destructively,"* he explained.

23   Hector went inside to rinse his paintbrushes, and Logan contemplated what the old man had told him. A few minutes later, Logan joined Hector at the sink. "How do you release your emotions if you have no artistic abilities?" he asked. As he had the day before, Hector winked and left Logan standing alone, filled with questions.

24   When Logan arrived home, his mother yelled at him for forgetting to take the trash out. Later, his father grounded him because of the poor results of his history exam. Retiring to his room for the night, Logan noticed that his sister's hamster had chewed a hole through one of his new sneakers. Logan could feel his anger building, but just as he was about to explode, he caught a glimpse of the wooden figurine on his desk.

25   Taking a deep breath, Logan thought of Hector. *Do something constructive, not destructive,* he said to himself. Looking around his room, Logan spied his guitar in the corner. He hadn't touched it in years, but something inside told him to pick it up and play. Sitting on the corner of his bed, he rested the guitar on his lap and began plucking the strings. Instantly, the storm that had been building inside him dissipated, and his shoulders relaxed.

26   Logan played cards with Hector in the Recreation Room the next day, and they exchanged stories about their families and friends. At the end of the hour, Logan hoisted his backpack and guitar case onto his shoulders, said goodbye, and started to walk away. When he reached the door, he turned around and winked at Hector.

27   "Thanks," he said.

? Questions

4 According to the story, which of the following **best** describes Hector?

 A enterprising

 B frustrated

 C confused

 D shy

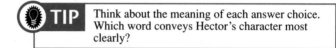

TIP Think about the meaning of each answer choice. Which word conveys Hector's character most clearly?

5 According to the story, how does Hector know that Logan is a troublemaker?

 A He sees Logan carrying a backpack.

 B He knows Logan plays the guitar.

 C He is at the nursing home after school.

 D He sees Logan's black eye.

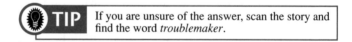

TIP If you are unsure of the answer, scan the story and find the word *troublemaker*.

6 The author notes that Logan winks at Hector at the end of the story. What is the writer suggesting?

 A He has shared a secret with Hector.

 B He is trying to make Hector laugh.

 C Hector usually winks at him.

 D Hector is trying to be constructive.

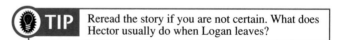

TIP Reread the story if you are not certain. What does Hector usually do when Logan leaves?

Passage 3

Read the following passage. Then answer the questions that follow. Use the Tip below each question to help you choose the correct answer. When you finish, read the answer explanations at the end of this chapter.

Excerpt from *Winesburg, Ohio*
by Sherwood Anderson

1   Young George Willard got out of bed at four in the morning. It was April and the young tree leaves were just coming out of their buds. The trees along the residence streets in Winesburg are maple and the seeds are winged. When the wind blows they whirl crazily about, filling the air and making a carpet underfoot.

2   George came downstairs into the hotel office carrying a brown leather bag. His trunk was packed for departure. Since two o'clock he had been awake thinking of the journey he was about to take and wondering what he would find at the end of his journey. The boy who slept in the hotel office lay on a cot by the door. His mouth was open and he snored lustily. George crept past the cot and went out into the silent deserted main street. The east was pink with the dawn and long streaks of light climbed into the sky where a few stars still shone.

3   Beyond the last house on Trunion Pike in Winesburg there is a great stretch of open fields. The fields are owned by farmers who live in town and drive homeward at evening along Trunion Pike in light creaking wagons. In the fields are planted berries and small fruits. In the late afternoon in the hot summers when the road and the fields are covered with dust, a smoky haze lies over the great flat basin of land. To look across it is like looking out across the sea. In the spring when the land is green the effect is somewhat different. The land becomes a wide green billiard table on which tiny human insects toil up and down.

4   All through his boyhood and young manhood George Willard had been in the habit of walking on Trunion Pike. He had been in the midst of the great open place on winter nights when it was covered with snow and only the moon looked down at him; he had been there in the fall when bleak winds blew and on summer evenings when the air vibrated with the song of insects. On the April morning he wanted to go there again, to walk again in the silence. He did walk to where the road dipped down by a little stream two miles from town and then turned and walked silently back again. When he got to Main Street clerks were sweeping the sidewalks before the stores. "Hey, you George. How does it feel to be going away?" they asked.

5   The westbound train leaves Winesburg at seven forty-five in the morning. Tom Little is conductor. His train runs from Cleveland to where it connects with a great trunk line railroad with terminals in Chicago and New York. Tom has what in railroad circles is called an "easy run." Every evening he returns to his family. In the fall and spring he spends his Sundays fishing in Lake Erie. He has a round red face and small blue eyes. He knows the people in the towns along his railroad better than a city man knows the people who live in his apartment building.

6   George came down the little incline from the New Willard House at seven o'clock. Tom Willard carried his bag. The son had become taller than the father.

7   On the station platform everyone shook the young man's hand. More than a dozen people waited about. Then they talked of their own affairs. Even Will Henderson, who was lazy and often slept until nine, had got out of bed. George was embarrassed. Gertrude Wilmot, a tall thin woman of fifty who worked in the Winesburg post office, came along the station platform. She had never before paid any attention to George. Now she stopped and put out her hand. In two words she voiced what everyone felt. "Good luck," she said sharply and then turning went on her way.

8   When the train came into the station George felt relieved. He scampered hurriedly aboard. Helen White came running along Main Street hoping to have a parting word with him, but he had found a seat and did not see her. When the train started Tom Little punched his ticket, grinned and, although he knew George well and knew on what adventure he was just setting out, made no comment. Tom had seen a thousand George Willards go out of their towns to the city. It was a commonplace enough incident with him. In the smoking car there was a man who had just invited Tom to go on a fishing trip to Sandusky Bay. He wanted to accept the invitation and talk over details.

9   George glanced up and down the car to be sure no one was looking, then took out his pocket-book and counted his money. His mind was occupied with a desire not to appear green. Almost the last words his father had said to him concerned the matter of his behavior when he got to the city. "Be a sharp one," Tom Willard had said. "Keep your eyes on your money. Be awake. That's the ticket. Don't let anyone think you're a greenhorn."

10   After George counted his money he looked out of the window and was surprised to see that the train was still in Winesburg.

11   The young man, going out of his town to meet the adventure of life, began to think but he did not think of anything very big or dramatic. Things like his mother's death, his departure from Winesburg, the uncertainty of his future life in the city, the serious and larger aspects of his life did not come into his mind.

12   He thought of little things—Turk Smollet wheeling boards through the main street of his town in the morning, a tall woman, beautifully gowned, who had once stayed overnight at his father's hotel, Butch Wheeler the lamp lighter of Winesburg hurrying through the streets on a summer evening and holding a torch in his hand, Helen White standing by a window in the Winesburg post office and putting a stamp on an envelope.

13   The young man's mind was carried away by his growing passion for dreams. One looking at him would not have thought him particularly sharp. With the recollection of little things occupying his mind he closed his eyes and leaned back in the car seat. He stayed that way for a long time and when he aroused himself and again looked out of the car window the town of Winesburg had disappeared and his life there had become but a background on which to paint the dreams of his manhood.

? Questions

7   The narrator notes George's behavior after he finds himself alone in the car. What is the narrator suggesting?

   A   George has not brought enough money for his trip.

   B   George is slightly nervous about leaving his hometown.

   C   George thinks Tom Little took too much money from him.

   D   George is tired and wants to take a nap on the train.

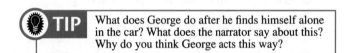

TIP What does George do after he finds himself alone in the car? What does the narrator say about this? Why do you think George acts this way?

8   Explain why George gets up so early to walk down Trunion Pike. Use relevant and specific information from the excerpt to support your answer.

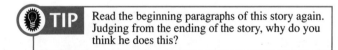

TIP Read the beginning paragraphs of this story again. Judging from the ending of the story, why do you think he does this?

9 Based on the story, which of the following **best** explains how George feels about Winesburg?

   A He wishes he did not have to leave the small town.

   B He wants to remember the small town when he leaves.

   C He wishes more people would have come to say goodbye.

   D He wants to make the town better for its inhabitants.

 First, eliminate any answers that are obviously wrong. Then think about George's final hours in the town. What do his actions convey about his feelings for the town?

10 Based on the excerpt, which of the following **best** explains how Tom Little feels about George leaving Winesburg?

   A He is indifferent to George's departure.

   B He is happy that George is going somewhere.

   C He is jealous that George is leaving.

   D He is sad to see George leaving indefinitely.

 Reread the paragraph that included Tom Little. Think about his actions and how they are described.

Passage 4

Read the following passage. Then answer the questions that follow. Use the Tip below each question to help you choose the correct answer. When you finish, read the answer explanations at the end of this chapter.

Excerpt from "The Hypnotist"
by Ambrose Bierce

1   My first knowledge that I possessed unusual powers came to me in my fourteenth year, when at school. Happening one day to have forgotten to bring my noon-day luncheon, I gazed longingly at that of a small girl who was preparing to eat hers. Looking up, her eyes met mine and she seemed unable to withdraw them. After a moment of hesitancy she came forward in an absent kind of way and without a word surrendered her little basket with its tempting contents and walked away. Inexpressibly pleased, I relieved my hunger and destroyed the basket. After that I had not the trouble to bring a luncheon for myself: that little girl was my daily purveyor. . . . The girl was always persuaded that she had eaten all herself; and later in the day her tearful complaints of hunger surprised the teacher, entertained the pupils, earned for her the sobriquet of Greedy-Gut and filled me with a peace past understanding. . . .

2   For some years afterward I had little opportunity to practice hypnotism; such small essays as I made at it were commonly barren of other recognition than solitary confinement on a bread-and-water diet; sometimes, indeed, they elicited nothing better than the cat-o'-nine-tails. It was when I was about to leave the scene of these small disappointments that my one really important feat was performed.

3   I had been called into the warden's office and given a suit of civilian's clothing, a trifling sum of money and a great deal of advice, which I am bound to confess was of a much better quality than the clothing. As I was passing out of the gate into the light of freedom I suddenly turned and looking the warden gravely in the eye, soon had him in control.

4   "You are an ostrich," I said.

5   At the post-mortem examination the stomach was found to contain a great quantity of indigestible articles mostly of wood or metal. Stuck fast in the esophagus and constituting, according to the Coroner's jury, the immediate cause of death, one door-knob.

6   I was by nature a good and affectionate son, but as I took my way into the great world from which I had been so long secluded I could not help remembering that all my misfortunes had flowed like a stream from . . . my parents in the matter of school luncheons; and I knew of no reason to think they had reformed. . . .

7   It was while going afoot to South Asphyxia, the home of my childhood, that I found both my parents on their way to the Hill. They had hitched their team and were eating luncheon under an oak tree in the center of the field. The sight of the luncheon called up painful memories of my school days and roused the sleeping lion in my breast.

8   Approaching the guilty couple, who at once recognized me, I ventured to suggest that I share their hospitality.

9   "Of this cheer, my son," said the author of my being, with characteristic pomposity, which age had not withered, "there is sufficient for but two. I am not, I hope, insensible to the hunger-light in your eyes, but—"

10   My father has never completed that sentence; what he mistook for hunger-light was simply the earnest gaze of the hypnotist. In a few seconds he was at my service. A few more sufficed for the lady, and the dictates of a just resentment could be carried into effect. "My former father," I said, "I presume that it is known to you that you and this lady are no longer what you were?"

11   "I have observed a certain subtle change," was the rather dubious reply of the old gentleman; "it is perhaps attributable to age."

12   "It is more than that," I explained; "it goes to character—to species. You and the lady here are, in truth, two broncos—wild stallions both, and unfriendly."

13   "Why, John," exclaimed my dear mother, "you don't mean to say that I am—"

14   "Madam," I replied, solemnly, fixing my eyes again upon hers, "you are."

15   Scarcely had the words fallen from my lips when she dropped upon her hands and knees, and backing up to the old man squealed like a demon and delivered a vicious kick upon his shin! An instant later he was himself down on all-fours, headed away from her and flinging his feet. . . . With equal earnestness but inferior agility, because of her hampering body-gear, she plied her own. Their flying legs crossed and mingled in the most bewildering way. . . . On recovering themselves they would resume the combat, uttering their frenzy in the nameless sounds of the furious brutes which they believed themselves to be—the whole region rang with their clamor! . . . Wild, inarticulate screams of rage attested the delivery of the blows; groans, grunts and gasps their receipt. Nothing more truly military was ever seen at Gettysburg or Waterloo: the valor of my dear parents in the hour of danger can never cease to be to me a source of pride and gratification. . . .

16 Arrested for provoking a breach of the peace, I was, and have ever since been, tried in the Court of Technicalities and Continuances whence, after fifteen years of proceedings, my attorney is moving heaven and earth to get the case taken to the Court of Remandment for New Trials.

17 Such are a few of my principal experiments in the mysterious force or agency known as hypnotic suggestion. Whether or not it could be employed by a bad man for an unworthy purpose I am unable to say.

Questions

11 Based on the excerpt, which of the following **best** explains how the narrator feels about his parents?

   A He forgives them for their mistakes.

   B He thinks they did a great job raising him.

   C He feels that they are incredibly intelligent.

   D He is mad at them for not being generous.

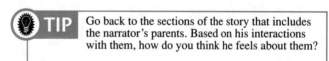

> **TIP** Go back to the sections of the story that includes the narrator's parents. Based on his interactions with them, how do you think he feels about them?

12 The narrator notes that whether his powers can be used for an "unworthy purpose" he is "unable to say." What is the narrator poking fun at?

   A his dissatisfaction with his powers

   B his parents' punishment of him

   C the usefulness of his experiment

   D his lack of remorse for his actions

> **TIP** Eliminate answer choices that are obviously incorrect. Then think about the final statement the narrator makes. How does it change your understanding of the story?

13   In this story, why does the author use a first-person point of view?

     A   so readers sympathize with the narrator's plight

     B   so the narrator doesn't realize how bad his actions are

     C   so the parents are shown in a very positive light

     D   so the story is not told in the correct order

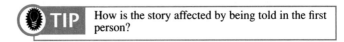

> **TIP**   How is the story affected by being told in the first person?

14   According to the story, which of the following **best** describes the narrator?

     A   happy-go-lucky

     B   sluggish

     C   short-tempered

     D   fortunate

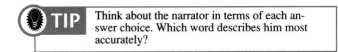

> **TIP**   Think about the narrator in terms of each answer choice. Which word describes him most accurately?

 Answers

1   C

Pete spent most of the time trying to create luck for the test.

2   A

The words *no excuses* are italicized to emphasize that the warning is serious.

3   D

Pete does not seem lazy because he does quite a bit to prepare for the test. He does not seem annoyed, and in light of this story's ending, his actions are not very clever. The best word to describe Pete is *foolish*.

4   A

Because Hector is so good at finding ways to channel his emotions, he might be called enterprising.

5   D

Hector says that he gets all the troublemakers. Plus, Logan has a black eye.

6   A

Hector usually winks at Logan before he leaves. The wink suggests that the two have shared a secret.

7   B

George counts his money because he wants to protect it and himself so he does not "appear green" on his trip. Because he is recalling his father's advice and taking inventory of what he's brought, readers can assume he is slightly nervous about his impending trip.

8   Sample answer

In the beginning of the story, George states that "all through his boyhood and young manhood . . . [he] had been in the habit of walking on Trunion Pike." Because he is leaving his small town, he is revisiting one of the significant places where he spent his childhood. The fact that he wants to see this again before he leaves suggests that he is leaving for good and does not plan to see Trunion Pike again.

It is also significant that George says he used to come here in the snow, when the moon would be his only company. This seems to suggest that despite all the friendly characters in Winesburg, George sometimes felt alone in the small town. In a way, this foreshadows the way he feels at the end of the story: ready to depart and experience a new place.

9 **B**

George's actions in his final hours definitely show that he wants to remember the small town. Also, during his departure, he does not daydream about his next adventure but about the subtle aspects of the town. This shows his sentimentality for the town. However, his actions also imply that he is excited to leave.

10 **A**

Tom Little smiles at George when he punches his ticket, showing that he doesn't have any ill will toward George. However, Tom is described as having sent thousands of Georges on their way and is eager to discuss the details of his upcoming fishing trip. Thus, he is indifferent to George's leaving.

11 **D**

The narrator mentions in the middle of the story that he blames his parents' not giving him big enough lunches for the horrible things he does in his life. His later treatment of his parents when they will not share their picnic reiterates his anger at them.

12 **D**

The final statement by the narrator conveys how he has no remorse for his actions. Such an ironic statement sheds a humorous light on all the narrator's previous actions.

13 **B**

Because this story is told in the first person, the actions of the narrator are presented as if they are justified instead of ridiculous. From the last line of the story, readers can tell that the narrator has no concept of how bad his actions really are.

14 **C**

When the narrator does not like the way he is treated, he reacts very strongly and very quickly. This is the mark of someone who is short-tempered.

Chapter 5

Poetry

Standard 14: Students will identify, analyze, and apply knowledge of the theme, structure, and elements of poetry and provide evidence from the text to support their understanding.

14.5 Identify, respond to, and analyze the effects of sound, form, figurative language, graphics, and dramatic structure of poems:

- Sound (alliteration, onomatopoeia, rhyme scheme, consonance, assonance)
- Form (ballad, sonnet, heroic couplets)
- Figurative language (personification, metaphor, simile, hyperbole, symbolism)
- Dramatic structure

Elements of Poetry

Questions on the MCAS for this standard will be on poetry passages. These questions ask about elements of poetry, such as sound, form, figurative language, and dramatic structure. They may be multiple-choice or open-response questions.

Some questions for this standard might ask you to interpret the meaning of selected lines in a poem. Other questions might ask you about a more specific choice the poet has made—for instance, the idea the author conveys by choosing to use a certain word or phrase in a poem. Many of these questions will ask you to choose the poetry technique an author uses to convey a certain point.

You might also be asked to identify metaphors or similes in the passages as well as instances of personification, hyperbole, and symbolism. You might be asked to identify the effects of sound—for example, alliteration, onomatopoeia, rhyme scheme, consonance, and assonance. Questions on this standard might ask you to identify the form of a poem, such as ballad, sonnet, or heroic couplet.

Passage 1

Read the following excerpt from a poem. Then answer the questions that follow. Use the Tip below each question to help you choose the correct answer. When you finish, read the answer explanations at the end of this chapter.

Excerpt from *Beowulf*

1 You have heard of the Danish Kings

in the old days and how

they were great warriors.

Shield, the son of Sheaf,

5 took many an enemy's chair,

terrified many a warrior,

after he was found an orphan.

He prospered under the sky

until people everywhere

10 listened when he spoke.

He was a good king!

(?) Questions

1 What does the poet **most likely** mean when he writes in line 5 that the king "took many an enemy's chair"?

  A He stole his enemies' belongings.

  B He forgave many of his enemies.

  C He dethroned many of his enemies.

  D He helped many of his enemies.

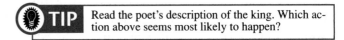

TIP Read the poet's description of the king. Which action above seems most likely to happen?

2　How does the poet help readers understand that his subject was a "good king"?

　　A　by listing details

　　B　by using short lines

　　C　by saying he was an orphan

　　D　by using a historical setting

 Of the answer choices listed, which one best proves that the subject of the poem was a "good king"?

3　What does the poet describe in lines 1, 2, and 3?

　　A　the work of another famous poet

　　B　the history of an area

　　C　the lives of his parents

　　D　a war between warriors and kings

 Read the lines over and over until you can make sense of what the poet is trying to say. Then pick the answer that best sums up what the lines describe.

Passage 2

Read the following poem. Then answer the questions that follow. Use the Tip below each question to help you choose the correct answer. When you finish, read the answer explanations at the end of this chapter.

I Wandered Lonely as a Cloud
by William Wordsworth

1   I wandered lonely as a cloud

     That floats on high o'er vales and hills,

     When all at once I saw a crowd,

     A host, of golden daffodils,

5   Beside the lake, beneath the trees

     Fluttering and dancing in the breeze.

     Continuous as the stars that shine

     And twinkle on the Milky Way,

     They stretched in never-ending line

10 Along the margin of a bay:

     Ten thousand saw I at a glance

     Tossing their heads in sprightly dance.

     The waves beside them danced, but they

     Out-did the sparkling waves in glee:

15 A poet could not but be gay

     In such a jocund company:

     I gazed—and gazed—but little thought

     What wealth the show to me had brought.

For oft, when on my couch I lie

20 In vacant or in pensive mood,

They flash upon that inward eye

Which is the bliss of solitude;

And then my heart with pleasure fills

And dances with the daffodils.

Questions

4   What does the speaker mean when he says in lines 15 and 16, "A poet could not but be gay / In such a jocund company"?

A   The sight is so uplifting, it makes him happy.

B   The smell is so strong, it makes him tired.

C   There are so many flowers that he feels lonely.

D   The flowers are so bright that he has a headache.

> **TIP** If you do not know the meaning of some of the words used in the poem, read the rest of the poem and try to understand the context. How does to speaker feel about what he is writing about? Which answer choice seems most likely?

5   What does the author describe in line 12?

   A   the way the ladies danced

   B   the way the clouds shifted

   C   the way the flowers moved

   D   the way the stars sparkled

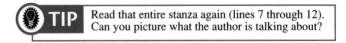 Read that entire stanza again (lines 7 through 12). Can you picture what the author is talking about?

6   What simile does the speaker use for the amount of flowers he sees?

   A   clouds in the sky

   B   hills in the valley

   C   stars in the galaxy

   D   waves in the ocean

 Look for each answer choice in the poem. Then figure out what the poet is comparing the image to. Of the answer choices, which image does the speaker use to describe the amount of daffodils that he sees?

Passage 3

Read the following excerpt from a poem. Then answer the questions that follow. Use the Tip below each question to help you choose the correct answer. When you finish, read the answer explanations at the end of this chapter.

Excerpt from *Don Juan*
by Lord Byron

1   Don Jose and the Donna Inez led

    For some time an unhappy sort of life,

    Wishing each other, not divorced, but dead;

    They lived respectably as man and wife,

5   Their conduct was exceedingly well-bred,

    And gave no outward signs of inward strife,

    Until at length the smother'd fire broke out,

    And put the business past all kind of doubt.

    For Inez call'd some druggists and physicians,

10 And tried to prove her loving lord was mad;

    But as he had some lucid intermissions,

    She next decided he was only bad;

    Yet when they ask'd her for her depositions,

    No sort of explanation could be had,

15 Save that her duty both to man and God

    Required this conduct—which seem'd very odd.

    She kept a journal, where his faults were noted,

    And open'd certain trunks of books and letters,

    All which might, if occasion served, be quoted;

20 And then she had all Seville for abettors,

    Besides her good old grandmother (who doted);

    The hearers of her case became repeaters,

    Then advocates, inquisitors, and judges,

    Some for amusement, others for old grudges.

(?) Questions

7 What does the speaker mean when he says in line 11, "he had some lucid intermissions"?

   A Most of the time he was fun to be around.

   B There were times when he was sane.

   C He thoroughly enjoyed the theater.

   D He was never nice to his wife.

 Read the stanza in which this line appears. Paraphrase the events in the stanza. Which answer choice correlates with what you think went on in the stanza?

8 What does the speaker describe in lines 23 and 24?

   A the couple's many roles within the marriage

   B the people who have never heard of the couple

   C outsiders who gossip about and judge the couple

   D the lawyers who defend the couple in court

 The final lines of the poem describe certain people in the story of the husband and wife. Who are the people these lines describe?

9 What metaphor does the speaker use for the relationship between Don Jose and Donna Inez?

   A a controlled fire

   B doctor and patient

   C a court case

   D an amusement park

 Reread the poem and look for instances of the speaker making a metaphor about the relationship.

10 How does the poet help readers understand that the speaker is not on the wife's side?

   A by presenting the poem in the past tense

   B by using an intricate rhyme scheme

   C by writing about her in third person

   D by using humor to describe her actions

 Of the answer choices, which helps you to understand that the speaker does not take the complaints of the wife seriously?

Passage 4

Read the following poem. Then answer the questions that follow. Use the Tip below each question to help you choose the correct answer. When you finish, read the answer explanations at the end of this chapter.

Ulysses

Alfred Lord Tennyson

  1   It little profits that an idle king,

        By this still hearth, among these barren crags,

        Match'd with an aged wife, I mete and dole

        Unequal laws unto a savage race,

  5   That hoard, and sleep, and feed, and know not me.

        I cannot rest from travel: I will drink

        Life to the lees: all times I have enjoy'd

        Greatly, have suffer'd greatly, both with those

        That loved me, and alone; on shore, and when

 10   Thro' scudding drifts the rainy Hyades

        Vest the dim sea: I am become a name;

        For always roaming with a hungry heart

        Much have I seen and known; cities of men

        And manners, climates, councils, governments,

 15   Myself not least, but honour'd of them all;

        And drunk delight of battle with my peers;

        Far on the ringing plains of windy Troy.

        I am part of all that I have met;

        Yet all experience is an arch wherethro'

 20   Gleams that untravell'd world, whose margin fades

        For ever and for ever when I move.

        How dull it is to pause, to make an end,

        To rust unburnish'd, not to shine in use!

        As tho' to breath were life. Life piled on life

25   Were all to little, and of one to me

        Little remains: but every hour is saved

        From that eternal silence, something more,

        A bringer of new things; and vile it were

        For some three suns to store and hoard myself,

30   And this gray spirit yearning in desire

        To follow knowledge like a sinking star,

        Beyond the utmost bound of human thought.

        This is my son, mine own Telemachus,

        To whom I leave the sceptre and the isle—

35   Well-loved of me, discerning to fulfill

        This labour, by slow prudence to make mild

        A rugged people, and thro' soft degrees

        Subdue them to the useful and the good.

        Most blameless is he, centred in the sphere

40   Of common duties, decent not to fail

        In offices of tenderness, and pay

        Meet adoration to my household gods,

        When I am gone. He works his work, I mine.

        There lies the port; the vessel puffs her sail:

45   There gloom the dark broad seas. My mariners,

        Souls that have toil'd, and wrought, and thought with me—

        That ever with a frolic welcome took

        The thunder and the sunshine, and opposed

        Free hearts, free foreheads—you and I are old;

50   Old age had yet his honour and his toil;

        Death closes all: but something ere the end,

        Some work of noble note, may yet be done,

        Not unbecoming men that strove with Gods.

        The lights begin to twinkle from the rocks:

55 The long day wanes: the slow moon climbs: the deep

Moans round with many voices. Come, my friends,

'Tis not too late to seek a newer world.

Push off, and sitting well in order smite

The sounding furrows; for my purpose holds

60 To sail beyond the sunset, and the baths

Of all the western stars, until I die.

It may be that the gulfs will wash us down:

It may be we shall touch the Happy Isles,

And see the great Achilles, whom we knew.

65 Tho' much is taken, much abides; and tho'

We are not now that strength which in the old days

Moved earth and heaven; that which we are, we are;

One equal-temper of heroic hearts,

Made weak by time and fate, but strong in will

70 To strive, to seek, to find, and not to yield.

Questions

11 Explain how the poem builds to its concluding stanza. Use relevant and specific information from the poem to support your answer.

TIP This question is asking you to explain how the final stanza works in the poem. The question implies that the final stanza makes some sort of final statement on the stanzas that came before it. Explain how the final stanza adds to the meaning of this poem.

12 What does the speaker mean when he says in lines 19 and 20, "Yet all experience is an arch wherethro' / Gleams that untravell'd world"?

   A His experiences are enough to make him happy.

   B Experiences are like lessons that we learn.

   C His experiences remind him that he wants to do more.

   D Experiences leave a person feeling unfulfilled.

 Think about the words and try to create an image in your mind of what the author is trying to say. Visualizing the metaphors poets use often helps readers understand complex ideas.

13 What is conveyed by the speaker's shift from talking about himself to his son in lines 33 through 43?

   A The speaker blames his son for not being free to leave home.

   B All people have certain responsibilities they must fulfill.

   C The speaker fears his son will not be a good leader.

   D Most people want to be king, but the speaker does not.

 Read the lines about the speaker's son very slowly until you have a clear understanding of what the speaker is trying to say.

14 What does the poet **most likely** mean when he writes "a hungry heart" in line 12?

   A the declining beauty of his aged wife

   B the soothing calm of old age

   C the craving for adventure

   D the excitement of sacrifice

 Read the section of the poem where the speaker mentions "a hungry heart." Judging from the context of the words, what do you think the phrase means?

 **Answers**

1   C

Because the poem is about being a successful warrior and king, the poet most likely means that his subject conquered and took the place (or dethroned) many of his enemies.

2   A

Although the poet does use short lines, this in no way proves that the subject of the poem was a good king. Answer choices C and D also have no bearing on whether the subject was a good king. The correct answer is A.

3   B

The poet is referencing the history of the area to give readers a basis for the story he is about to tell.

4   A

The speaker is saying that the sight of the daffodils blowing in the breeze fills him with such an uplifting feeling that he cannot help but feel extremely happy.

5   C

In line 12, the author is describing the way the flowers moved. After describing how they stretch on seemingly forever, he compares their movement to a dance.

6   C

The poet compares himself to a cloud in the sky. Though he describes the hills in the valley and the waves in the ocean, he does not use them as similes for something else. The speaker compares the amount of daffodils to the "continuous . . . stars that shine . . . on the Milky Way."

7   B

In the stanza, the wife tries proving that her husband is insane, but when he has periods of sanity, or "some lucid intermissions," she changes her mind.

8   C

These lines describe the roles of the people who gossip about the couple's problems even though they are outside the relationship—people who take sides without knowing the whole story.

9   A

In the first stanza, the speaker describes an unhappy marriage that is kept under wraps. However, at the end of that stanza, the speaker explains, "Until at length the smother'd fire broke out," comparing the relationship to a controlled fire.

10 D

Answer choices A, B, and C are elements in the poem: the poem is in the present tense, it has an intricate rhyme scheme, and it is told in the third person. However, the only element listed that helps readers to see that the speaker is not on the wife's side is that the speaker treats the wife's complaints as if they were humorous instead of serious.

11 Sample answer

This poem builds to its concluding stanza by telling a story throughout the prior stanzas that is summed up in the final stanza. In this poem, the final stanza works like a concluding paragraph in an essay: the last stanza summarizes the point of the entire poem.

Earlier in the poem, the speaker says that now that he has come to the end of a grand and dangerous adventure, he is reaping the rewards of spending quiet time with his wife at his home. He says that though this is what he worked so hard for, he misses the excitement and danger of life. The speaker describes the exciting adventures of traveling and fighting. Now, having come to a point in his life where he does not see any danger in his future, he is bored.

The final stanza reiterates this point by comparing modern people with people of the past. The speaker is saying that earlier generations always had bigger adventures than the current adventure. He also seems to be saying that people grow less strong in time, but their drive for adventure and the danger of an exciting life remains vibrant.

12 C

The speaker is saying that going on adventures does not kill the urge that humans have to experience life. Instead of being satisfied by his memories of his life, he is reminded that he wishes he could do more.

13 B

Answer choices A and C do not work because the speaker does not blame his son and does think he will make a good king when he is gone. The speaker also looks quite favorably on his life, so we have no reason to think he does not want to be king. Lines 33 through 43 seem to imply that all people have responsibilities in their lives that they must fulfill, even if they would rather be doing other things.

14 C

The phrase "hungry heart" is an expression the poet uses to mean the king's craving for adventure. His heart is hungry for more exciting experiences.

Chapter 6

Myth, Classical Literature, and Drama

Standard 16: Students will identify, analyze, and apply knowledge of the themes, structure, and elements of myths, traditional narratives, and classical literature and provide evidence from the text to support their understanding.

16.11 Analyze the characters, structure, and themes of classical Greek drama and epic poetry.

Standard 17: Students will identify, analyze, and apply knowledge of the themes, structure, and elements of drama and provide evidence from the text to support their understanding.

17.7 Identify and analyze how dramatic conventions support, interpret, and enhance dramatic text.

Classical Literature

The term *classical literature* refers to narratives, poetry, and drama written in ancient Greece, ancient Rome, and other ancient civilizations. This broad period, known as classical antiquity, ranges from about the seventh century BCE to the fifth century CE. Literary works common to the period include myths, epic poetry, and dramas.

Myth

A myth is a story that explains the beliefs of a culture. The myths of ancient Greece, Rome, and other ancient cultures most often center on the religious figures of the time. Ancient cultures believed in polytheism, the worship of many gods, or deities. Ancient mythology presents stories of the lives of the gods and goddesses, as well as the heroic adventures of important mortal figures, in narrative form. In these stories, deities often interact with and affect the lives of the culture's mythological heroes. Myths can also function to explain how something came to be the way it is today.

Epic Poetry

An epic is a long, narrative poem that tells about the actions and accomplishments of a legendary or historical hero. Typically, the hero of an epic embarks on a dangerous journey—often involving a war—and faces many hardships before arriving at a specific destination. In many epics, gods and goddesses both help and hinder the hero as he travels. The outcome of the journey rarely affects the hero himself but more often decides the fate of an entire culture. Epic heroes are challenged and tested when they encounter evil temptations and physically improbable feats. A hero who ultimately passes these tests serves as an example of proper moral conduct. In this way, epics often provide readers with a sense of the cultural values of a group of people.

Theme in Classical Literature

The theme of a literary work is the topic or subject addressed by the work. Some common themes in classical literature deal with fate, war, human strengths and weaknesses, heroic deeds, and the battle between good and evil. These themes are conveyed through the speech, actions, and thoughts of a work's characters.

Dramatic Conventions

Dramatic conventions are the standards or rules that generally guide playwrights, producers, and audiences in the creation and viewing of theatrical productions. Each type of play has its own conventions. For example, in a tragedy, the hero or heroine is often caught in unfortunate or disastrous circumstances that he or she cannot control, while in a comedy, the hero or heroine usually starts out in a bad situation, but he or she ultimately prevails.

Passage 1

Read the following passage. Then answer the questions that follow. Use the Tip below each question to help you choose the correct answer. When you finish, read the answer explanations at the end of this chapter.

Se-Osiris and the Sealed Scroll
adapted from an Egyptian myth

1 For as long as anyone, even the oldest of the sages, could remember, the great kingdoms of Egypt and Ethiopia had been locked in competition. In Egypt, many successive pharaohs and generation upon generation of citizens spent their lives feeling great contempt for the Ethiopians. The Ethiopians, in turn, were insulted by the Egyptians' arrogance and became preoccupied with outdoing their proud neighbors.

2 It seemed inevitable that this bitter contest would someday culminate in a great battle—if not by swords and chariots then by magic.

3 Ramses the Great reigned in Egypt during a period of increased tension with the Ethiopians. One evening, as he tended to duties in his palace, his chief advisor, the Grand Vizier, rushed to his side. "Pharaoh, there is an Ethiopian wizard here. He requests an audience with you immediately."

4   Ramses' face turned as serious as stone as he consented to meet with the wizard. The Grand Vizier hurried to the antechamber and opened the door. An imposing Ethiopian wizard, standing nearly as tall as the ceiling, entered. He shouldered his way past the Grand Vizier and headed directly to Ramses.

5   The Ethiopian bowed curtly before the Egyptian pharaoh and held up a tightly rolled, sealed scroll of papyrus. "King of Egypt," he said, "the wizards of Ethiopia have mastered the ability to read sealed letters and scrolls. I have here a scroll that is duly sealed. If none of your magicians can read it as it is, without breaking the seal, then I will have proved the superiority of the magicians of Ethiopia."

6   Ramses was concerned but endeavored not to show it. He accepted the challenge, asserting that there surely must be an Egyptian wizard who could surpass the abilities of the weak, cowardly Ethiopians. Then, he dismissed the wizard, telling him to return the next day for the promised showdown. Smiling with sly confidence, the wizard turned and departed.

7   Ramses was left with a problem that even he, the great king of Egypt, found overwhelming. He immediately called a counsel with all the most powerful wizards of Egypt. One by one he interviewed them, and one by one they shrank from the challenge. Regardless of the extent of their powers or the significance of their accomplishments, none would dare try to magically read a scroll without unrolling it.

8   Dejected, Ramses retired to his chamber. As he reclined, feeling the weight of many burdens, he barely noticed the patter of small feet on the floor. Looking up, he saw his grandson, Se-Osiris, standing nearby. Though only twelve, Se-Osiris had a reputation as a talented fledgling magician. Regarding his grandfather now, Se-Osiris seemed to sense the older man's troubles.

9   "Pharaoh, what is the matter?" asked the boy, sitting on the edge of the couch. Ramses hesitantly explained the severity of his problem and expressed his doubt that any Egyptian was equal to the task at hand.

10   Strangely, Se-Osiris only laughed. Ramses, startled by the boy's apparent impudence, shook him. "What is the meaning of this laughter?" he demanded.

11   "Pharaoh, I don't laugh to mock you. I laugh out of joy. This challenge is a blessing, for it will finally allow the kingdom of Egypt to prove its superiority over Ethiopia." When Ramses looked at the boy with puzzlement, Se-Osiris continued, "Pharaoh, Grandfather, *I* can read that scroll!"

12   Ramses scowled at his grandson's brash claim and waved him away. "Leave me alone with my troubles," he said gravely.

13   The following day, the entire court gathered to observe the scheduled meeting with the Ethiopian wizard. The wizard stood before the pharaoh to restate his claim; no other Egyptians dared stand near them, except for young Se-Osiris.

14   Again, the Ethiopian wizard held his scroll aloft. "King of Egypt, the wizards of Ethiopia are able to read scrolls that are sealed. Can any wizard in your kingdom, or any peasant, or any Egyptian at all, meet such a challenge?" When the only person to step forward was Se-Osiris, the Ethiopian laughed. "Is *this* all you have to offer?"

15   Se-Osiris closed his eyes and concentrated, just for a moment. The words on the scroll were delivered magically to his mind, and he began slowly and clearly reciting them. As Se-Osiris spoke, the Ethiopian looked less and less confident until his immense shoulders were slouched and his eyes were wide with disbelief. It was clear to the entire court and Ramses that the boy was reciting, word for word, the contents of the sealed scroll.

16   Even more shocking and alarming to the listeners were the revelations in the ancient scroll's text. The scroll outlined the ancient competition between Egypt and Ethiopia. Five hundred years ago, the great Ethiopian wizard Kherheb had used his magic to humiliate a pharaoh, an ancestor of Ramses. Then, in turn, Kherheb was humiliated.

17   As the story continued, it became clear to the listeners that the Ethiopian wizard who stood before them was none other than Kherheb himself, restlessly scouring the world for ways to take further vengeance on Egypt.

18   But on that day, neither the wizards of Ethiopia nor the king of Egypt had a victory. The victory went to an amazing boy named Se-Osiris.

? Questions

1   In the myth, what does the reader learn from Se-Osiris's discussion with Ramses?

A   Egypt and Ethiopia are locked in competition.

B   Even the Pharaoh had no faith in Se-Osiris.

C   The Pharaoh lives in an elegant palace.

D   Only Ethiopian wizards can read sealed scrolls.

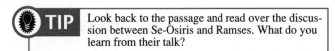

TIP   Look back to the passage and read over the discussion between Se-Osiris and Ramses. What do you learn from their talk?

2   In paragraph 14, the Ethiopian wizard challenges "any wizard in your kingdom, or any peasant, or any Egyptian at all." What does this suggest about him?

A   He used to live in Egypt long ago.

B   He is uncertain of his own abilities.

C   He has sympathy for the pharaoh.

D   He views his challenge on a national scale.

 TIP Read the wizard's challenge again, and think about how he acted in the story. When he includes so many people in his challenge, what is he trying to do?

3   Read these lines from paragraph 10 of the myth.

Ramses, startled by the boy's apparent impudence, shook him. "What is the meaning of this laughter?" he demanded.

What does Ramses think when the boy laughs?

A   The boy is mocking him.

B   The boy is confident in his magic.

C   The boy fears the Ethiopians.

D   The boy does not understand the problem.

 TIP Read the answer choices carefully. Think about Ramses' reaction to the boy's laughter. Also, look at the words in the sentence for hints.

Passage 2

In the Greek epic poem *The Aeneid*, the Trojan hero Aeneas tells the tale of the destruction of the city of Troy by his enemies, the Greeks. Read the following excerpt from the poem. Then answer the questions that follow. Use the Tip below each question to help you choose the correct answer. When you finish, read the answer explanations at the end of this chapter.

Excerpt from *The Aeneid*
by Virgil

1   Now peals of shouts come thund'ring from afar,

   Cries, threats, and loud laments, and mingled war:

   The noise approaches, tho' our palace stood.

   Aloof from streets, encompass'd with a wood.

5   Louder, and yet more loud, I hear th' alarms

   Of human cries distinct, and clashing arms.

   Fear broke my slumbers; I no longer stay,

   But mount the terrace, thence the town survey,

   And hearken what the frightful sounds convey.

10   Thus, when a flood of fire by wind is borne,

   Crackling it rolls, and mows the standing corn;

   Or deluges, descending on the plains,

   Sweep o'er the yellow year, destroy the pains

   Of lab'ring oxen and the peasant's gains;

15   Unroot the forest oaks, and bear away

   Flocks, folds, and trees, and undistinguish'd prey:

   The shepherd climbs the cliff, and sees from far

   The wasteful ravage of the wat'ry war.

   Then Hector's faith was manifestly clear'd,

20   And Grecian frauds in open light appear'd.

   The palace of Deiphobus ascends

In smoky flames, and catches on his friends.

Ucalegon burns next: the seas are bright

With splendor not their own, and shine with Trojan light.

25 New clamors and new clangors now arise,

The sound of trumpets mix'd with fighting cries.

With frenzy seiz'd, I run to meet th' alarms,

Resolv'd on death, resolv'd to die in arms,

But first to gather friends, with them t' oppose

30 (If fortune favor'd) and repel the foes;

Spurr'd by my courage, by my country fir'd,

With sense of honor and revenge inspir'd.

(?) Questions

4   In line 13, what does the speaker mean when he says "yellow year"?

A   a year to be feared

B   a year's worth of thriving corn crops

C   a year of bad health

D   a year's worth of sun-bleached grass

 Read the lines just before and after this line. What images does the poet want the reader to see? What is he describing in this line?

5 In line 28, the speaker says that he is "resolv'd on death, resolv'd to die in arms." What does this suggest about him?

    A He wishes that his wife would be there to hold him when he dies in battle.

    B He is predicting that many of his friends will die before the battle is over.

    C He would rather kill his enemies and die himself than live without fighting.

    D He is so pained by the fire that he wishes for death because he will never recover.

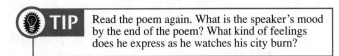
TIP   Read the poem again. What is the speaker's mood by the end of the poem? What kind of feelings does he express as he watches his city burn?

6 In the poem, what does the fire symbolize?

    A the changing of seasons

    B the corruption of palace rulers

    C the chance to start over again

    D the powerful destruction of war

TIP   What is happening in the poem? Read the poem again and consider what is taking place. What might the fire in the poem symbolize?

Passage 3

In this scene from The *Importance of Being Earnest,* you will see a conversation between two of the main characters in the play. This conversation reveals important things about these characters. Read the excerpt from Oscar Wilde's play. Then answer the questions that follow. Use the Tip below each question to help you choose the correct answer. When you finish, read the answer explanations at the end of this chapter.

Excerpt from *The Importance of Being Earnest*
by Oscar Wilde

Morning-room in Algernon's flat in Half-Moon Street. The room is luxuriously and artistically furnished.

1   ALGERNON   How are you, my dear Ernest? What brings you up to town?

JACK   Oh, pleasure, pleasure! What else should bring one anywhere? Eating as usual, I see, Algy!

ALGERNON (*Stiffly.*)   I believe it is customary in good society to take some slight refreshment at five o'clock. Where have you been since last Thursday?

JACK (*Sitting down on the sofa.*)   In the country.

5   ALGERNON   What on earth do you do there?

JACK (*Pulling off his gloves.*)   When one is in town one amuses oneself. When one is in the country one amuses other people. It is excessively boring.

ALGERNON   And who are the people you amuse?

JACK (*Airily.*)   Oh, neighbours, neighbours.

ALGERNON   Got nice neighbours in your part of Shropshire?

10   JACK   Perfectly horrid! Never speak to one of them.

ALGERNON   How immensely you must amuse them! (*Goes over and takes a sandwich.*) By the way, Shropshire is your county, is it not?

JACK   Eh? Shropshire? Yes, of course. Hallo! Why all these cups? Why cucumber sandwiches? Why such reckless extravagance in one so young? Who is coming to tea?

ALGERNON   Oh! merely Aunt Augusta and Gwendolen.

JACK   How perfectly delightful!

15   ALGERNON   Yes, that is all very well; but I am afraid Aunt Augusta won't quite approve of your being here.

JACK   May I ask why?

ALGERNON   My dear fellow, the way you flirt with Gwendolen is perfectly disgraceful. It is almost as bad as the way Gwendolen flirts with you.

JACK   I am in love with Gwendolen. I have come up to town expressly to propose to her.

ALGERNON   I thought you had come up for pleasure? . . . I call that business.

20   JACK   How utterly unromantic you are!

ALGERNON   I really don't see anything romantic in proposing. It is very romantic to be in love. But there is nothing romantic about a definite proposal. Why, one may be accepted. One usually is, I believe. Then the excitement is all over. The very essence of romance is uncertainty. If ever I get married, I'll certainly try to forget the fact.

JACK   I have no doubt about that, dear Algy. The Divorce Court was specially invented for people whose memories are so curiously constituted.

ALGERNON   Oh! there is no use speculating on that subject. Divorces are made in Heaven—(JACK *puts out his hand to take a sandwich.* ALGERNON *at once interferes.*) Please don't touch the cucumber sandwiches. They are ordered specially for Aunt Augusta. (*Takes one and eats it.*)

JACK   Well, you have been eating them all the time.

25   ALGERNON   That is quite a different matter. She is my aunt. (*Takes plate from below.*) Have some bread and butter. The bread and butter is for Gwendolen. Gwendolen is devoted to bread and butter.

JACK (*Advancing to table and helping himself.*)   And very good bread and butter it is too.

ALGERNON   Well, my dear fellow, you need not eat as if you were going to eat it all. You behave as if you were married to her already. You are not married to her already, and I don't think you ever will be.

JACK   Why on earth do you say that?

ALGERNON   Well, in the first place girls never marry the men they flirt with. Girls don't think it right.

30   JACK   Oh, that is nonsense!

ALGERNON   It isn't. It is a great truth. It accounts for the extraordinary number of bachelors that one sees all over the place. In the second place, I don't give my consent.

JACK   Your consent!

ALGERNON   My dear fellow, Gwendolen is my first cousin. And before I allow you to marry her, you will have to clear up the whole question of Cecily. (_Rings bell._)

JACK   Cecily! What on earth do you mean? What do you mean, Algy, by Cecily! I don't know any one of the name of Cecily.

35   (_Enter_ LANE)

ALGERNON   Bring me that cigarette case Mr. Worthing left in the smoking-room the last time he dined here.

LANE   Yes, sir. (LANE _goes out._)

JACK   Do you mean to say you have had my cigarette case all this time? I wish to goodness you had let me know. I have been writing frantic letters to Scotland Yard about it. I was very nearly offering a large reward.

ALGERNON   Well, I wish you would offer one. I happen to be more than usually hard up.

40   JACK   There is no good offering a large reward now that the thing is found.

(_Enter_ LANE _with the cigarette case on a salver._ ALGERNON _takes it at once._ LANE _goes out._)

ALGERNON   I think that is rather mean of you, Ernest, I must say. (_Opens case and examines it._) However, it makes no matter, for, now that I look at the inscription inside, I find that the thing isn't yours after all.

JACK   Of course it's mine. (_Moving to him._) You have seen me with it a hundred times, and you have no right whatsoever to read what is written inside. It is a very ungentlemanly thing to read a private cigarette case.

ALGERNON   Oh! it is absurd to have a hard and fast rule about what one should read and what one shouldn't. More than half of modern culture depends on what one shouldn't read.

45   JACK   I am quite aware of the fact, and I don't propose to discuss modern culture. It isn't the sort of thing one should talk of in private. I simply want my cigarette case back.

ALGERNON   Yes; but this isn't your cigarette case. This cigarette case is a present from some one of the name of Cecily, and you said you didn't know any one of that name.

? Questions

7   In the excerpt, what does the reader learn from Algernon's conversation with Jack?

A   Jack has given Algernon a false name.

B   Algernon is in love with Cecily.

C   Jack has a habit of losing things.

D   Algernon does not like living in the country.

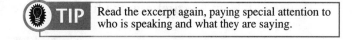

TIP Read the excerpt again, paying special attention to who is speaking and what they are saying.

8   In line 27, Algernon tells Jack, "you need not eat as if you were going to eat it all." What does this line suggest?

A   Algernon thinks that Jack always eats too much food when he visits.

B   Algernon thinks that Jack is helping himself to whatever he wants.

C   Algernon is afraid that no food will be left for his aunt and cousin.

D   Algernon wants to keep all the cucumber sandwiches for himself.

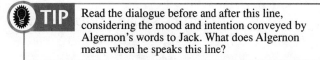

TIP Read the dialogue before and after this line, considering the mood and intention conveyed by Algernon's words to Jack. What does Algernon mean when he speaks this line?

9 Read these sentences (line 34) from the excerpt.

> Cecily! What on earth do you mean? What do you mean, Algy, by Cecily! I don't know any one of the name of Cecily.

What is the effect of the repetition of the name Cecily?

A It shows that Jack does not know a person with this name.

B It shows that Jack is trying not to forget the name.

C It shows that Jack cannot recall who might have this name.

D It shows that Jack is nervous at the mention of the name.

 TIP Reread this line and the lines that follow. Picture the characters as they are engaged in the scene. Why did the author choose to use repetition here? What does Jack's reaction reveal about him?

10 At the end of the excerpt, what does Algernon learn about Jack?

A He is forgetful.

B He does not really love Gwendolen.

C He is lying to Algernon.

D He will be more careful in the future.

 TIP Consider what has happened in this excerpt. What does Algernon know about Jack at the end of the excerpt that he did not know in the beginning?

Passage 4

The Greek epic *The Odyssey* tells the story of Odysseus, king of Ithaca, and the events of his ten-year journey home after the Trojan War. After suffering many hardships, Odysseus and his men land on the Aegean Islands, home of the goddess and sorceress Circe. Read the following excerpt and then answer the questions that follow. Use the Tip below each question to help you choose the correct answer. When you finish, read the answer explanations at the end of this chapter.

Excerpt from *The Odyssey*
by Homer (translated by Samuel Butler)

1   "When they reached Circe's[1] house they found it built of cut stones, on a site that could be seen from far, in the middle of the forest. There were wild mountain wolves and lions prowling all round it—poor bewitched creatures whom she had tamed by her enchantments and drugged into subjection. They did not attack my men, but wagged their great tails, fawned upon them, and rubbed their noses lovingly against them. As hounds crowd round their master when they see him coming from dinner—for they know he will bring them something—even so did these wolves and lions with their great claws fawn upon my men, but the men were terribly frightened at seeing such strange creatures.

2   "Presently they reached the gates of the goddess's house, and as they stood there they could hear Circe within, singing most beautifully as she worked at her loom, making a web so fine, so soft, and of such dazzling colours as no one but a goddess could weave. On this Polites, whom I valued and trusted more than any other of my men, said, 'There is someone inside working at a loom and singing most beautifully; the whole place resounds with it, let us call her and see whether she is woman or goddess.'

3   "They called her and she came down, unfastened the door, and bade them enter. They, thinking no evil, followed her, all except Eurylochus, who suspected mischief and staid outside. When she had got them into her house, she set them upon benches and seats and mixed them a mess with cheese, honey, meal, and Pramnian wine, but she drugged it with wicked poisons to make them forget their homes, and when they had drunk she turned them into pigs by a stroke of her wand, and shut them up in her pigstyes. They were like pigs—head, hair, and all, and they grunted just as pigs do; but their senses were the same as before, and they remembered everything.

4   "Thus then were they shut up squealing, and Circe threw them some acorns and beech masts such as pigs eat, but Eurylochus hurried back to tell me about the sad fate of our comrades. He was so overcome with dismay that though he tried to speak he could find no words to do so; his eyes filled with tears and he could only sob and sigh, till at last we forced his story out of him, and he told us what had happened to the others. . . .

5   "With this I left the ship and went up inland. When I got through the charmed grove, and was near the great house of the enchantress Circe, I met Mercury[2] with his golden wand, disguised as a young man in the hey-day of his youth and beauty with the down just coming upon his face. He came up to me and took my hand within his own, saying, 'My poor unhappy man, whither are you going over this mountain top, alone and without knowing the way? Your men are shut up in Circe's pigstyes, like so many wild boars in their lairs. You surely do not fancy that you can set them free? I can tell you that you will never get back and will have to stay there with the rest of them. But never mind, I will protect you and get you out of your difficulty. Take this herb, which is one of great virtue, and keep it about you when you go to Circe's house, it will be a talisman to you against every kind of mischief. . . .'

6   "When I got to the gates I stood there and called the goddess, and as soon as she heard me she came down, opened the door, and asked me to come in; so I followed her—much troubled in my mind. She set me on a richly decorated seat inlaid with silver, there was a footstool also under my feet, and she mixed a mess in a golden goblet for me to drink; but she drugged it, for she meant me mischief. When she had given it me, and I had drunk it without its charming me, she struck me with her wand. 'There now,' she cried, 'be off to the pigstye, and make your lair with the rest of them.'

7   "But I rushed at her with my sword drawn as though I would kill her, whereon she fell with a loud scream, clasped my knees, and spoke piteously, saying, 'Who and whence are you? From what place and people have you come? How can it be that my drugs have no power to charm you? Never yet was any man able to stand so much as a taste of the herb I gave you; you must be spell-proof; surely you can be none other than the bold hero Ulysses,[3] who Mercury always said would come here some day with his ship while on his way home from Troy; so be it then; sheathe your sword and let us . . . make friends and learn to trust each other.'

8   "And I answered, 'Circe, how can you expect me to be friendly with you when you have just been turning all my men into pigs? . . . You must free my men and bring them to me that I may see them with my own eyes.'

9   "When I had said this she went straight through the court with her wand in her hand and opened the pigstye doors. My men came out like so many prime hogs and stood looking at her, but she went about among them and anointed each with a second drug, whereon the bristles that the bad drug had given them fell off, and they became men again, younger than they were before, and much taller and better looking. They knew me at once, seized me each of them by the hand, and wept for joy till the whole house was filled with the sound of their halloa-ballooing, and Circe herself was so sorry for them that she came up to me and said, 'Ulysses, noble son of Laertes, go back at once to the sea where you have left your ship, and first draw it on to the land. Then, hide all your ship's gear and property in some cave, and come back here with your men. . . . I know how much you have all of you suffered at sea, and how ill you have fared among cruel savages on the mainland, but that is over now, so stay here, and eat and drink till you are once more as strong and hearty as you were when you left Ithaca; for at present you are weakened both in body and mind; you keep all the time thinking of the hardships you have suffered during your travels, so that you have no more cheerfulness left in you.'

10 "We stayed with Circe for a whole twelvemonth feasting upon an untold quantity both of meat and wine. But when the year had passed in the waning of moons and the long days had come round, my men called me apart and said, 'Sir, it is time you began to think about going home, if so be you are to be spared to see your house and native country at all. . . .'

11 The goddess listened to what I had got to say. 'Circe,' said I, 'please to keep the promise you made me about furthering me on my homeward voyage. I want to get back and so do my men. . . .'

12 "And the goddess answered, 'Ulysses, noble son of Laertes, you shall none of you stay here any longer if you do not want to, but there is another journey which you have got to take before you can sail homewards. You must go to the house of Hades.[4] . . .'"

1. *Circe* = sorceress and enchantress; daughter of Helios, the sun god.

2. *Mercury* = messenger to the gods; patron of travelers, merchants, rogues, and thieves.

3. *Ulysses* = Latin name for Odysseus.

4. *House of Hades* = the underworld; world of the dead.

⑦ Questions

11 In the myth, what does Circe's singing symbolize?

    A a false sense of security

    B a desire for companionship

    C a willingness to reform

    D a longing for a better life

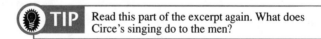

TIP Read this part of the excerpt again. What does Circe's singing do to the men?

12 What does the reader learn from Circe's speech in paragraph 7?

    A Circe is not going to let Odysseus live.

    B Circe is in love with Odysseus.

    C Circe is angry with Mercury.

    D Circe is not used to being tricked.

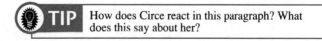

TIP How does Circe react in this paragraph? What does this say about her?

13 In the myth, what does the god Mercury symbolize?

   A the foolishness of mortal beings

   B the possibility of triumph over evil

   C the harmony of man and his environment

   D the power of the art of disguise

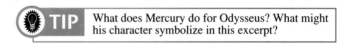

TIP What does Mercury do for Odysseus? What might his character symbolize in this excerpt?

14 In paragraph 5, what does Mercury mean when he says, "You surely do not fancy that you can set them free"?

   A Odysseus should leave the island at once.

   B Odysseus' men will be trapped forever.

   C Odysseus cannot beat Circe without help.

   D Odysseus' travels will end at the island.

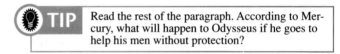

TIP Read the rest of the paragraph. According to Mercury, what will happen to Odysseus if he goes to help his men without protection?

✔ Answers

1 B

Although Se-Osiris bravely offers to help, the Pharaoh reacts with scorn. He thinks the boy is mocking him or being unrealistic. This discussion shows the reader that Ramses does not have faith in the ability of his grandson, Se-Osiris, to perform magic that could meet the Ethiopian's challenge.

2 D

The Ethiopian speaks as though the entire kingdom of Egypt could not produce a person—magician or not—who could match his feat. He shows scorn for the entire nation and challenges it.

3 A

When Se-Osiris laughs about the Ethiopian's magic challenge, Ramses suspects that the boy is mocking him. The text explains that Ramses was "startled by the boy's apparent impudence," which means he was stunned that the boy was so bold. The other answer choices do not accurately explain Ramses' reaction.

4 B

The lines before this line talk about the fire mowing the standing corn. The line after refers to the work of peasants and oxen to grow the corn. This leads readers to believe that the corn crop was thriving. The phrase "yellow year" refers to the year's worth of corn that was growing on the plains.

5 C

The phrase "in arms" here refers to bearing weapons. The speaker has armed himself to bring death to his enemies. He is aware of the fact that in the process, he may also die, but this does not stop him. The speaker's mood by the end of the poem is courageous and revengeful.

6 D

The fire is sweeping through the city, as is the war. As crops are consumed and buildings fall, we can assume from the "clashing arms" and "human cries distinct" that soldiers are taking lives. Answer choice D is the best answer.

7 A

In the beginning of the excerpt, Algernon refers to Jack as Ernest, even though readers can tell that this is not his real name. He calls him Ernest again at line 42. Because of this, readers can tell that Jack has told Algernon that his name is Ernest. The other answer choices are not revealed in this excerpt.

8 B

Though this statement may appear to reflect Algernon's fear that there will not be any food left after Jack eats, Algernon is trying to tell Jack that he has no right to feel that he holds a comfortable place in the family. When Jack helps himself to the bread and butter that is meant for Gwendolen, Algernon interprets the action to mean that Jack is helping himself to both the food and Gwendolen.

9 D

Jack's repetition of the name Cecily indicates that he is hiding something from Algernon and his family. The first time Algernon mentions the name, Jack insistently denies knowing anyone named Cecily. Because readers already know that he is lying, this repetition is a sign that he is nervous because he fears he may soon be caught in a lie.

10 C

Algernon knows that the cigarette case belongs to Jack. When Jack denies knowing anyone by the name of Cecily, and then Algernon reads the inscription in the cigarette case, he knows that Jack is lying.

11 A

Circe's beautiful singing makes the men feel at ease and erases their suspicions that an evil force might be at work, as they thought when they saw the bewitched creatures outside of Circe's door. This sense of security is false, however, because they are soon drugged and turned into pigs.

12 D

Circe is shocked when she is unable to turn Odysseus, or Ulysses, into a pig, as though her magic has never once failed her before this time. She does not act as if she loves him or has a desire to kill him, nor does she seem to be angry with Mercury. Answer choice D is best.

13 B

With Mercury's help, Odysseus, or Ulysses, is able to overcome Circe's evil spell. Though Mercury thinks that Odysseus, a mortal, is foolish for thinking he might be able to do this on his own, Mercury himself does not represent this notion. While Mercury, a deity, seems to be in harmony with his environment, Odysseus, a mortal man, does not. Mercury's disguise as a younger version of himself does not relate to his role in the excerpt. Answer choice B is the best answer.

14 C

Mercury is telling Odysseus that he cannot expect to free his men without help, because he will meet the same fate. This is why Mercury helps him; to do it without Mercury's help would be impossible.

Chapter 7

Nonfiction

Standard 13: Students will identify, analyze, and apply knowledge of the purpose, structure, and elements of nonfiction or informational materials and provide evidence from the text to support their understanding.

> 13.24 Analyze the logic and use of evidence in an author's argument.

> 13.25 Analyze and explain the structure and elements of nonfiction works.

Author's Purpose

Authors write for many reasons. They may write short stories, novels, or poems to entertain their readers. They may write articles and nonfiction books that inform or describe something to readers. Some authors write political speeches and letters to editors to persuade their readers to think and act as they do about certain issues. Analyzing the author's choice of title and the examples or details used to support the main idea will help you to better understand a passage. Understanding the author's purpose will also help you decide whether the argument of the passage is logical and valid.

Structure and Elements

Be aware of the literary elements that an author chooses to use in a passage. Keep an eye out for word choice, sentence style, and to whom the author seems to be speaking. This will enable you to understand why the author uses certain devices in a selection and help you to determine whether those devices are effective.

Passage 1

Read the following passage. Then answer the questions that follow. Use the Tip underneath each question to help you choose the correct answer. When you finish, read the answer explanations at the end of this chapter.

Fuel of the Future
by Shelby Greene

1 Just because you don't see a biodiesel gas station on every street corner does not mean you cannot start incorporating this fuel into your life. With the cost of gas on the rise and politicians talking about a mandatory freeze on our use of fossil fuels, biodiesel—fuel partly manufactured from plants—is becoming a viable option for powering our vehicles. The government is generating all sorts of incentives to convince people to switch to biodiesel, including big tax breaks. Last year, U.S. production of biodiesel tripled. Politicians are getting behind biodiesel because it solves two of our nation's biggest problems:

- Americans can begin to break their addiction to fossil fuels.

- The struggling business of agriculture will get a huge boost from the sudden surge in demand.

2 The global-warming debate has been heating up lately since scientists have discovered more evidence of the dire effects of global warming. A greater reliance on biodiesel translates into less expulsion of greenhouse gases into the atmosphere.

Even if there are no biodiesel distributors near you, biodiesel works in any diesel engine. One small but significant step you can take is to buy a diesel car instead of a car that runs on traditional unleaded gasoline. When the green revolution goes into full swing, you will be ready. In field tests, cars powered by biodiesel have been shown to perform comparably to vehicles that run on traditional fuels. Contrary to what many people believe, biodiesel is distributed all over the United States, and the number of stations offering it is growing.

? Questions

1   Who is the author's intended audience?

   A   people shopping for a new car

   B   politicians who control our fuel supplies

   C   people using fuel in their daily lives

   D   environmentalists concerned about pollution

 TIP   Reread the article before you choose an answer. Then decide for whom the author wrote this article.

2   Based on the selection, what is the author's expectation about the future of biodiesel?

   A   Biodiesel will be used more often in the future.

   B   More people will begin buying diesel cars.

   C   Politicians will push for tax breaks for biodiesel distributors.

   D   Global warming will decrease through the use of biodiesel.

 TIP   Read the article again. What does the author seem to be saying about the use of biodiesel in the future?

3   Read this sentence from paragraph 2.

   When the green revolution goes into full swing, you will be ready.

   Which of the following statements is the best clarification of the meaning of this sentence?

   A   The reader needs to start using more environmentally friendly fuels now.

   B   The reader will be prepared when biodiesel replaces fossil fuel.

   C   The reader should expect to start buying biodiesel to save money.

   D   The reader will not be shocked when fossil fuels are no longer available.

 TIP   Read paragraph 2 one more time. Concentrate on the sentences surrounding the one in the box. What does this context tell you about the meaning of the sentence?

Passage 2

Read the following passage. Then answer the questions that follow. Use the Tip below each question to help you choose the correct answer. When you finish, read the answer explanations at the end of this chapter.

Tarantula Tamer

by Jacqueline Ray

1   If you ask Sidney Reich about her work, she will say her job is the greatest in the world, although most people would disagree. Sidney is a scientist specializing in the study and protection of the tarantula, a hairy creature that makes most people cringe.

2   Reich says her fascination with insects, particularly arachnids (insects with an exo-skeleton), began when she was just a little girl. "I spent my early childhood in a rural town in Pennsylvania, where they weren't many children to play with. To occupy my time, I roamed the woods near my home, carefully studying every daddy longlegs spider and tick I could find. I quickly observed that different types of spiders spun different types of webs, and I could seek out a spider simply by spotting its web. When I was about twelve, my family moved to California and I attended a much larger school. There I met many other kids who were interested in learning all about arachnids." Reich said she first saw a tarantula when hik-

ing with a friend. "I could not believe my eyes! It was monstrous—a good three or four inches long—and the most incredible arthropod I had ever seen." Reich explained that the tarantula did not reciprocate her interest and quickly scooted back into its burrow, but that didn't matter; she was already hooked and wanted to learn as much about tarantulas as possible.

3   Today Reich studies tarantulas in rain forests throughout the world. Because tarantulas are nocturnal, Reich observes them at night when they are active. When asked if her work is dangerous, Reich confesses that she has had a few close calls, but not with tarantulas. She has suffered several snakebites and even a scorpion bite. But Reich considers her suffering worthwhile if her research helps save tarantulas, some species of which are in danger of extinction. She explains that when most people see a tarantula, they are so frightened that they step on it and kill it on the spot. "People don't realize that there is no record of a human ever dying from a tarantula bite and that most tarantulas hide from people rather than attack them."

4   Reich blames horror movies for the tarantula's reputation as aggressive and deadly. The destruction of the rain forests is another factor affecting the tarantula population. "The more people learn about tarantulas, the better off the spiders will be," Reich concludes. "People will begin to appreciate tarantulas as an important part of nature and will not want to harm them."

? Questions

4   Which of the following is **most likely** the purpose of the passage?

   A   to persuade readers to get involved in a program to protect tarantulas

   B   to describe how a woman turned her fascination with spiders into a career

   C   to recommend that readers learn more about spiders to calm their fears

   D   to explain how tarantulas differ from the other species of spiders in the world

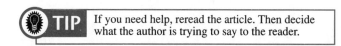

TIP   If you need help, reread the article. Then decide what the author is trying to say to the reader.

5   Based on the passage, which of the following is the **most likely** reason that tarantulas are feared by so many people?

   A   Tarantulas have displayed aggressive behavior towards humans.

   B   Tarantulas are known for being poisonous.

   C   Tarantulas are much larger than other species of spiders.

   D   Tarantulas have gotten a bad reputation from horror movies.

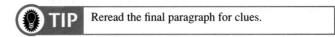 Reread the final paragraph for clues.

6   Which of the following **best** explains why Reich decided to study tarantulas?

   A   Reich investigated spiders as a child.

   B   Reich wants to educate people about tarantulas.

   C   Reich wanted to have an exciting career.

   D   Reich is trying to save tarantulas from extinction.

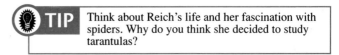 Think about Reich's life and her fascination with spiders. Why do you think she decided to study tarantulas?

Passage 3

Read the following passage. Then answer the questions that follow. Use the Tip below each question to help you choose the correct answer. When you finish, read the answer explanations at the end of this chapter.

A Rose by Any Other Name:
The Debate over the "Real" Shakespeare

1 William Shakespeare is thought to be one of the finest writers the world has ever known. His sonnets, tragedies, and comedies have captured the hearts and minds of readers across the globe. Though he is certainly one of literature's most beloved writers, he is also one of the most mysterious. Shakespeare both fascinates and frustrates historical scholars because very little is known about his personal life. Again and again, experts investigate the few pieces of evidence that have survived since the Elizabethan era. This probing has led many to question whether William Shakespeare wrote the plays that he has been credited with or if he even existed at all.

2 This heated debate is based on a number of inconsistencies in Shakespeare's biography. The first reason many experts question his identity is that very little historical documentation of his life exists. Even the most obscure figures in history have left some sort of paper trail investigators can follow to verify or disprove the existence of a person. In Shakespeare's case, only three documents bear his signature, with various spellings of the Bard's surname, and a handful of playbills list him as an actor in some shows. No letters, journals, or other type of personal correspondence backs up the Bard's identity as the master playwright.

3 People also list Shakespeare's background as another reason for suspicion. As the son of a community official, Shakespeare did not have the opportunities that members of the upper class enjoyed. Although little is known about his formal education, scholars of Shakespeare's dramatic works believe that the author of such plays would have needed a great knowledge of history and the ability to read both Latin and Greek. The lack of information about Shakespeare's schooling adds fuel to the debate.

4 So the question remains, if Shakespeare was not the author of some of the greatest plays ever penned, who was? Several theories exist about who the actual playwright was. One of the most popular ideas is that the name William Shakespeare was a pseudonym for Edward De Vere, the seventeenth earl of Oxford. It is thought that De Vere had to hide his true identity because many of the Shakespearean plays mock the British monarchy, with which De Vere was intimately acquainted. Opponents of this idea note that several of Shakespeare's plays were written after De Vere's death, though the dates of the plays are often disputed.

5 Other Shakespeare suspects include Sir Francis Bacon, a philosopher and lawyer, and Christopher Marlowe, a famous playwright. Some claim that Mary Sidney Herbert, countess of Pembroke was the real author but was forced by social conventions of the period to publish under a man's name. Most of these candidates are members of the upper class or aristocracy, making them well educated and well traveled, two qualities that many feel would have been essential to the author of Shakespeare's plays.

6   However, supporters of the Bard argue that Shakespeare's social status had little to do with his abilities as a writer. They point out that many of the world's greatest writers were self-taught and possessed raw talent rather than cultivated intellects. These supporters also look to the plays themselves to validate Shakespeare's identity. All the plays have the unique ability to transcend class and were loved by both courtiers and common people. Therefore, Shakespeare supporters contend, the plays could have been written by a middle-class man.

7   Of course, until conclusive proof is discovered, the controversy over the true identity of Shakespeare will continue. Still, many people feel "the play's the thing" and that authorship has little bearing on these wonderful works.

(?) Questions

7   Explain the significance of the article's title, "A Rose by Any Other Name: The Debate over the "Real" Shakespeare." Use relevant and specific information from the passage to support your answer.

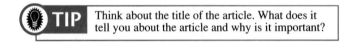

TIP   Think about the title of the article. What does it tell you about the article and why is it important?

8   According to the passage, what is the **most likely** reason that Shakespeare might not be the actual author of his plays and poems?

A   Shakespeare had very little formal education.

B   Some other historical figures most likely penned these works.

C   Some of Shakespeare's plays were published after his death.

D   There is no information on Shakespeare's personal life.

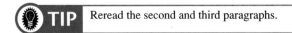

TIP   Reread the second and third paragraphs.

9 Which of the following is **most likely** the purpose of the passage?

   A to explain what historians have discovered about Shakespeare's life and works

   B to recommend that the reader study Shakespeare's contemporaries

   C to persuade the reader to investigate this controversy further

   D to describe the controversy surrounding the authorship of Shakespeare's works

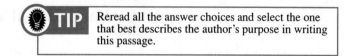

TIP Reread all the answer choices and select the one that best describes the author's purpose in writing this passage.

10 Read this sentence from paragraph 7.

> Still, many people feel "the play's the thing" and that authorship has little bearing on these wonderful works.

Which of the following does the sentence **most likely** mean?

   A Shakespeare's true identity has an effect on his works.

   B More investigation into the controversy is needed.

   C Shakespeare's identity does not devalue the work.

   D More investigation will not sway Shakespeare supporters.

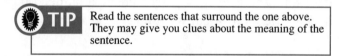

TIP Read the sentences that surround the one above. They may give you clues about the meaning of the sentence.

Passage 4

Read the following passage. Then answer the questions that follow. Use the Tip below each question to help you choose the correct answer. When you finish, read the answer explanations at the end of this chapter.

Don't Sweat Global Warming

1   Recently, scientists have suggested that Earth is experiencing its warmest temperatures in more than a thousand years. This is fascinating and important news, but it has many people concerned. Some of these people view global warming as a major problem and want emergency laws to be passed to help reduce it. However, I believe that these people's concerns are unnecessary. Passing new global-warming laws would do more harm than good to our world.

2   For several decades, scientists and concerned citizens have been exploring a theory called the greenhouse effect. This theory holds that the warming of the planet is caused by human activity. Factories, automobiles, and certain household appliances cause harmful gases to drift into the sky. Some of these pollutants are called greenhouse gases. They supposedly gather in the atmosphere and trap heat. Acting like a giant greenhouse, these gases cause the earth to grow warmer.

3   Believing greenhouse gases to be a main cause of global warming, many companies and countries joined together to reduce the amount of greenhouse gases they can legally emit. However, since then, leaders all over the world have begun to question the wisdom of this decision. The laws they passed create a burden on companies worldwide and are not having a clear effect on global warming.

4   Clearly, the planet *is* getting warmer. Average temperatures rise each year, and instances of record-breaking heat are more and more common. Also, there have been many unusual occurrences in the weather that may be tied to this warming, such as floods, droughts, and storms.

5   What is *not* clear is that human beings are the cause of this warming. I feel that greenhouse gases and other types of air pollution, while being dangerous and harmful to our planet, are not the cause of global warming. In fact, global warming is probably caused by Earth itself. Throughout the history of the world, temperatures have changed, sometimes significantly. There were times of blistering heat, as well as freezing Ice Ages, long before humans even existed. There was even a "mini Ice Age" as recently as a few hundred years ago. The Earth's temperature simply changes for reasons that are far beyond people's control.

6　People who still believe that greenhouse gases cause global warming have been pushing for new laws to reduce the gases. These laws would be aimed at changing the fuels we use and regulating, or even shutting down, businesses that emit greenhouse gases.

7　If these laws are passed, it would be a disaster for our economy. The laws would force many important businesses to stop production while they removed greenhouse gases from their factories. The "cleanup" could take weeks or months, and during that time the companies could lose millions of dollars. Meanwhile, consumers would be deprived of the companies' products.

8　Additionally, laws restricting emissions of greenhouse gases could have downright devastating effects on many foreign economies. The United States has many computer-based technological businesses that would not be altered by these laws. However, many other nations, especially developing ones, *rely* on factories. If their factories were shut down, these countries would lose an essential part of their economy and society. This would be tragic, especially because most greenhouse gases are produced by the United States and other, wealthier nations. Less fortunate countries would be made to suffer for the mistakes and misdeeds of Americans. Is that fair?

9　Even if these laws were put into effect and the world economy survived them, there is no guarantee that the laws would yield any positive results. Let's say that alternative sources of fuel and energy that do not produce greenhouse gases are put into widespread use. Who can say if these fuels will be effective? Also, almost every kind of fuel will have some harmful byproduct. Just because one type of energy does not leave behind greenhouse gases doesn't mean it is safe for the environment. For instance, nuclear power leaves behind poisonous nuclear wastes; even the so-called cleanest energies, solar and wind power, require the deforestation of large amounts of land. No kind of power is perfect, and the fuels that cause greenhouse gases are by no means the worst.

10　Despite these many reasonable objections to laws restricting the use of greenhouse gas, many people continue to push for them. These people insist that greenhouse gases cause global warming, and that global warming will culminate in global disaster. This idea has no foundation at all. As mentioned earlier, the temperature on Earth rises and falls naturally. There are cold periods and warm periods that occur randomly and without any sort of human interference. Global warming is natural and will not destroy the planet or its inhabitants.

11　People are continually overestimating the possible dangers of global warming and the effects of greenhouse gases. They claim that the heating of the planet may cause diseases like malaria to spread, kill vegetation and the animals that rely on it, encourage wildfires, and melt the polar ice caps. The final point is considered the most dangerous. If the polar ice caps melted, more water would be added to the oceans, causing them to rise. This can cause massive, deadly floods and would have the potential to permanently cover entire countries with water. These claims sound compelling, but they aren't realistic.

12   The situation is nowhere near as bad as many people insist. As scientists learn more and more about the warming of our planet, they continually realize that the effects of the warming will not be so dangerous. Only minute changes will take place, even over the course of many hundreds of years. There will be no sudden catastrophes because of global warming.

13   Earth is indeed warming, but it is a slow and entirely natural process. Global warming will not lead to disasters, and it is not caused by anything humans are doing or failing to do. People can pass thousands of laws to regulate factories, cars, and any other human-made objects, but the laws will have no effect on global warming. They will only make life harder for the people of Earth.

(?) Questions

11 Based on the passage, what is the author's expectations about global warming?

   A Global warming can be reduced through laws that restrict greenhouse gas emissions.

   B Global warming is a natural process that will not destroy our planet.

   C Global warming will stop once people start making lifestyle changes.

   D Global warming could lead to an increase in natural disasters.

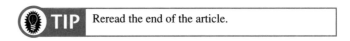
TIP Reread the end of the article.

12 Who is the author's intended audience for the passage?

   A politicians who make decisions concerning emissions

   B companies that produce greenhouse gases

   C scientists who argue that global warming is destroying our planet

   D people concerned about global warming

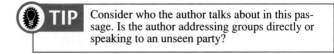
TIP Consider who the author talks about in this passage. Is the author addressing groups directly or speaking to an unseen party?

13 Based on the passage, which of the following **best** explains what the author thinks is the cause of global warming?

A Global warming is caused by the natural fluctuation of Earth's temperature.

B The greenhouse gases released by companies causes global warming.

C Global warming is caused by the nuclear power governments use to make weapons.

D Human beings' actions are the cause of global warming.

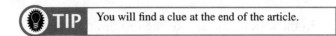

TIP You will find a clue at the end of the article.

14 In paragraphs 5 through 9, what writing technique does the author use to instruct the reader?

A He uses long, flowing sentences.

B He provides the reader with historical examples.

C He asks questions and then provides an answer.

D He addresses the reader directly.

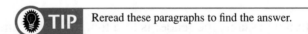

TIP Reread these paragraphs to find the answer.

✔ Answers

1 C

The passage is meant for people who use fuel (which includes most people), not for a specific group.

2 A

In the article, the author seems confident that biodiesel will replace the fossil fuels we use today. This is apparent in sentences like, "When the green revolution goes into full swing, you will be ready."

3 B

This sentence means that the reader will already be prepared for the changes that the common use of biodiesel will bring about.

4 B

This passage introduces the reader to Sidney Reich and provides the reader with information about her love of spiders and her interesting career.

5 D

In the passage, the reader is told that, "Reich blames horror movies for the tarantula's aggressive and deadly reputation."

6 D

The reader is told that despite her job's dangers, "Reich considers her suffering worthwhile if her research helps save tarantulas, some species of which are in danger of extinction."

7 Sample answer

The title "A Rose by Any Other Name: The Debate over the 'Real' Shakespeare" is significant because it directly addresses the controversy concerning the authorship of Shakespeare's works. The title, which includes a famous Shakespearean quote, asks the reader to question whether authorship matters. If it was discovered that Shakespeare's works had actually been written by someone of the upper class, like Edward De Vere, would this discovery change the meaning of the works? Would it have an effect on the way we read them? The title illustrates the underlying point of the passage, which forces the reader to question whether authorship matters and how it effects a work.

8   A

In paragraph 3, the author explains that little is known about Shakespeare's education. However, given his family's social status, it is likely that he had very little formal training. Many scholars question whether a person with little education would have had the ability to pen some of the greatest works of all time.

9   D

The author is merely explaining the controversy to the reader.

10   C

This sentence means that some people believe that the work is what is important, not who wrote it. Therefore, these people believe that the true identity of the author does not devalue the work in any way.

11   B

The author sees global warming as a natural process and has no expectations of imminent disaster.

12   D

The author seems to be speaking directly to people concerned about global warming because of all of the information they have heard from scientists and environmental groups over the years.

13   A

The author feels that global warming is caused by natural processes.

14   B

The author provides the reader with examples of Earth heating and cooling throughout history.

Chapter 8

Composition

Standard 19: Students will write with a clear focus, coherent organization, and sufficient detail.

19.30 Write coherent compositions with a clear focus, objective presentation of alternate views, rich detail, well-developed paragraphs, and logical argumentation.

Standard 20: Students will write for different audiences and purposes.

20.5 Use different levels of formality, style, and tone when composing for different audiences.

Standard 21: Students will demonstrate improvement in organization, content, paragraph development, level of detail, style, tone, and word choice (diction) in their compositions after revising them.

21.8 Revise writing by attending to topic/idea development, organization, level of detail, language/style, sentence structure, grammar and usage, and mechanics.

Standard 22: Students will use knowledge of Standard English conventions in their writing, revising, and editing.

22.9 Use knowledge of types of clauses (main and subordinate), verbals (gerunds, infinitives, participles), mechanics (semicolons, colons, hyphens), usage (tense consistency), sentence structure (parallel structure), and standard English spelling when writing and editing.

Standard 23: Students will organize ideas in writing in a way that makes sense for their purpose.

23.9 Integrate the use of organizing techniques that break up strict chronological order in a story (starting in the middle of the action, then filling in background information using flashbacks). For example, after reading the short story, "The Bet," by Anton Chekhov, students use flashbacks in their own stories and discuss the effect of this technique.

23.10 Organize information into a coherent essay or report with a thesis statement in the introduction, transition sentences to link paragraphs, and a conclusion.

Introduction

In this chapter, you will learn how to prepare for the written composition section of the MCAS. On the test, you will be asked to write an essay in response to a writing prompt. This chapter will help you develop your essay, paying special attention to its content and organization, sentence construction, usage, and writing mechanics. You will also be able to see how a composition written for the MCAS is graded and have the opportunity to look at a sample.

MCAS Writing Prompts

For the MCAS English Language Arts Composition test, you will be asked to write an essay in response to a writing prompt. MCAS writing prompts ask you to analyze works of literature, meaning that you will have to apply your knowledge of literary elements, themes, and structures in your composition.

The Composition section of the MCAS includes two test sessions, administered on the same day with a short break between sessions. During the first session, you will write an initial draft of a composition in response to the writing prompt. During the second session, you will revise your draft.

Hints for Taking the Composition Section of the MCAS

- Read the prompt carefully.
- Plan your writing by organizing your ideas.
- Support your ideas by providing details about each event, reason, or argument.
- Use a variety of sentence structures.
- Choose words that help others understand what you mean.
- Review and edit your writing.

Developing Your Essay

As you begin to develop your essay, remember the three stages of writing: prewriting, drafting, and revising. You should always begin to develop your essay by prewriting. Think about the audience you will be writing for and the purpose of your writing. Once you have determined your central idea, purpose, and audience, jot down some supporting material and organize or outline your ideas into a logical sequence. Then begin the drafting stage.

In the drafting stage, you will write a rough draft of your work. An important thing to remember when writing your draft is to get your ideas down on paper. This stage of your writing does not have to be perfect. It is acceptable for the rough draft to have mistakes. These mistakes can be changed or fixed in the final stage of writing: revising.

When your rough draft is finished, begin revising and editing your work. Read your rough draft carefully. Look for mistakes in grammar, spelling, punctuation, and capitalization. Look for sentence fragments. Make sure that you have stated your main idea or that you have provided enough supporting details for readers to determine the central theme. Reword sentences or move entire paragraphs to make your writing flow in a clear, logical order. Add more details to make your writing vibrant and exciting. When you are happy with your revised draft, write the final copy of your work in the answer booklet of your test.

Content and Organization

Your composition should be framed by strong opening and closing statements. Make sure that your opening addresses the reasons your topic is important and your conclusion states why you feel as you do about your topic.

Between the opening and closing of your composition are your main ideas. Make sure that your ideas are clear and that you have included a variety of main ideas and have not simply stressed the same point multiple times. Your ideas should follow a logical progression; that is, your transitions from one main idea to another should be smooth, not choppy, flowing easily from one idea to the next. Your ideas should also be supported by details, or reasons why you believe your ideas to be true. Also, be sure that you make smooth transitions from the opening of your essay to the main ideas to the closing.

Sentence Construction

Make sure that you follow traditional grammar rules when composing sentences. Check to make sure that you have placed periods and commas in logical places. Also make certain that all your sentences are not structured the same way. Variety will make your composition more interesting and more effective.

Usage

When you revise and edit, be sure to check that you have used correct verb tenses and agreements. For example, if you are writing about something that happened in the past, make certain that all the verbs you use to describe the past event are set in the past tense. Also, look at your pronouns (*I, you, he, she, it, we, they*) to make sure you have used them correctly. Examine your composition to verify that you have used words that will engage your audience. If you do not like the look or sound of a certain word in your composition, try to replace it with a better one.

Mechanics

Mechanics are the spelling, capitalization, and punctuation in your composition. If you are not sure of the spelling or capitalization of a word, look it up in a dictionary. You will not, however, be permitted to use a dictionary while taking the MCAS.

Practice MCAS Writing Prompt

> Often in works of literature, characters are surrounded by or associated with specific symbols or colors.
>
> From a work of literature you have read in or out of school, select a character that is surrounded by or associated with specific symbols or colors. In a well-developed composition, identify the character, describe the symbols or colors that surround the character, and explain why these symbols or colors are important to the work of literature.

How MCAS Compositions Are Graded

Your composition will be graded on the following six-point scale. A composition that receives six points is excellent.

Score	Description
6	• Rich topic/idea development
	• Careful and/or subtle organization
	• Effective/rich use of language
5	• Full topic/idea development
	• Logical organization
	• Strong details
	• Appropriate use of language
4	• Moderate topic/idea development and organization
	• Adequate, relevant details
	• Some variety in language
3	• Rudimentary topic/idea development and/or organization
	• Basic supporting details
	• Simplistic language
2	• Limited or weak topic/idea development, organization, and/or details
	• Limited awareness of audience and/or task
1	• Limited topic/idea development, organization, and/or details
	• Little or no awareness of audience and/or task

Sample Six-Point Composition

Remember the writing prompt you just read? The following is a sample response to this prompt. Notice that the sample clearly responds to the prompt. It contains good opening and closing statements and progresses logically from beginning to end. The essay is well developed and stays focused on the topic throughout. It contains few, if any, errors on usage, sentence construction, and mechanics. It sounds authentic and original and expresses the writer's individual or unique perspective.

Sample Answer

In the novel *The Great Gatsby*, the character of Daisy Buchanan is often surrounded or associated with the colors white and green. The flower for which Daisy is named is most often associated with the color white. Daisy is also described as wearing white throughout the novel. The color white is often associated with the ideas of innocence and naivety. Daisy is neither of these things, but she likes to pretend that she doesn't see or comprehend the damage that she does to the people around her. It seems that Daisy uses the color to hide all of the terrible parts of her life, so that it has the appearance of being perfect and clean. Other characters are seen wearing white in the novel, and every time, the color seems to be a way for the characters to gloss over all of the painful and ugly parts of their lives.

The color green is also associated with Daisy. Green is the color of money, and because Daisy is very wealthy, we often see her outside enjoying her lush green lawns. There is also a green light at the end of Daisy's dock. This symbolizes two different ideas in the novel. Jealousy is often referred to as "the green-eyed monster." Jay Gatsby, an old suitor of Daisy's, is jealous of the life that Daisy has with her rich husband. The green light at the end of the dock preoccupies Gatsby, almost taunting him by showing him the thing that he cannot have but desires the most, Daisy. When used in traffic lights, green means "go." Jay might see this as a sign that Daisy still has feeling for him and that he should try to win her back.

By surrounding Daisy with these colors, the author is giving the reader subtle clues about Daisy's true personality and what is to come. He uses the colors to show how hypocritical Daisy is and how she hides her true self from the world around her.

MCAS Grade 10, English Language Arts

Practice Test 1

Composition

WRITING PROMPT

In literature, characters sometimes make decisions that readers dislike or disagree with. From a work of literature you have read in or out of school, select a character who makes a decision that you disliked or disagreed with. In a well-developed composition, identify the character, describe the situation the character encountered and the decision he or she made, and explain how this decision affects the work of literature.

Go On

LANGUAGE AND LITERATURE: SESSION 1

This session contains three reading selections with sixteen multiple-choice questions and one open-response questions. Mark your answers to these questions in the spaces provided on your Answer Sheet.

In this article, author Sandy Miller discusses the history of yellow journalism, a type of writing that is sensational and not always accurate. Read "The Yellowed Pages of a Newspaper" to learn about yellow journalism. Answer the questions that follow.

The Yellowed Pages of a Newspaper

by **Sandy Miller**

1   Have you ever stood in line at the grocery store and rifled through the periodicals near the cash register? You might see some ordinary newspapers and maybe a few glossy fashion or home-decorating magazines. The headlines most likely to grab your attention, however, belong to the tabloids. These publications, which often contain stories about unidentified flying objects, alien babies, or celebrities who have returned from the dead, all have one thing in common: sensationalism. Tabloids tend to focus on stories of the bizarre, the unexplainable, or the extraordinary. Although these stories may be intriguing and suspenseful, they are usually quickly dismissed by readers and are certainly not considered good, concrete journalism. The sensationalistic—and sometimes even fabricated—stories in these types of publications are often referred to as yellow journalism. And believe it or not, yellow journalism actually began in the late nineteenth century with a competition between two of the leading daily newspapers in New York.

2   Though today his name is usually associated with the most prestigious award in American journalism, the Pulitzer Prize, Joseph Pulitzer was one of the men responsible for the creation of yellow journalism. Pulitzer was the owner of one of New York City's most successful dailies, the *New York World*. The paper's bold headlines and flamboyant approach to the news appealed to many readers, such as women, immigrants, and the poor. The ideas and opinions of these groups were often overshadowed in the other, more conservative, newspapers. The Sunday edition of the *New York World* even included a colorful comic strip called "Hogan's Alley," which featured a popular character whose bright yellow clothing earned him the name the "Yellow Kid."

3   The success of the *New York World* led the owners of other newspapers to imitate Pulitzer's daring new format. Among them was the owner of the *San Francisco Examiner*, William Randolph Hearst. As a student at Harvard, Hearst had worked on the university's newspa-

Go On

per. On leaving school, Hearst decided to make journalism his life's work. To prepare for this career, he served as an apprentice to Pulitzer at the *World*. Within a year, he had acquired his own newspaper, the struggling *San Francisco Examiner*, from his father. However, using Pulitzer's format, Hearst managed to transform the troubled paper into the best-selling newspaper in San Francisco.

4   Though Hearst had achieved success in California, he set his sights on a new challenge: owning the top daily newspaper in New York City. In 1895, he purchased the *New York Journal*, a small publication fighting to survive in the competitive New York market. Under Hearst's leadership, the *Journal* quickly became the *New York World's* biggest competition. In an effort to boost circulation, Hearst once again applied the bold approach to the news he had learned from Pulitzer. The headlines grew bigger and bolder, and the stories more sensational and suspenseful. Hearst lowered the price of the paper to just one penny, which even the poorest citizens of New York City could afford. In an even bolder move, Hearst enticed most of the staff of Pulitzer's *World*, including the creator of the "Hogan's Alley" comic strip, Richard Outcault, to leave their positions and work for the *Journal*.

5   Not to be outdone, Pulitzer replaced Outcault with a new artist to continue the "Hogan's Alley" comic strip. Conservative daily newspapers in New York witnessed the battle of the Yellow Kids and dubbed Hearst and Pulitzer's brand of reporting "yellow journalism." The term remains in use today to describe journalism that relies on glaring headlines and sensationalistic stories to sell subscriptions.

6   Perhaps the height of yellow journalism occurred during the Cuban Revolution, which eventually led to the Spanish-American War. Most newspapers try to approach the news objectively. They provide both sides of the story and let readers decide for themselves which side is right. However, Hearst's *Journal* clearly

stated its support for the Cuban revolutionaries fighting for their freedom from Spain. The *Journal's* stories about the injustices committed against Cuban citizens by the Spanish government supplied American readers with the scandalous material they had come to crave.

7   At the same time, the competition between Hearst and Pulitzer was growing fiercer, and neither man was willing to lose. In efforts to outdo each other, Hearst and Pulitzer did whatever they could to sell the most newspapers. They often lifted news right from the pages of their competitors. This practice would eventually contribute to the demise of Pulitzer's *New York World*. In 1898, Hearst caught Pulitzer in the act of stealing news from his newspaper. Hearst's *Journal* placed a fabricated story in the paper about the death of Colonel Reflipe W. Thenuz, which was Hearst's crafty way of saying, "We pilfer the news." The next day, the details of Thenuz's death were recounted in the pages of Pulitzer's *New York World*. This gave the *Journal* the ammunition it needed to sink the *World's* reputation.

8   Of course, Pulitzer wasn't the only yellow journalist guilty of questionable practices. According to legend, Hearst sent an illustrator to Cuba to capture the struggles of the Cuban citizens as they fought against Spanish control. Shortly after arriving in what he expected to be a war-torn country, the illustrator sent a cable to Hearst explaining that there was no war to cover. Supposedly, Hearst responded with his own cable: "You furnish the pictures. I'll furnish the war." Although Hearst steadfastly denied that this transmission ever took place, it has long been included in discussions of yellow journalism.

9   As the problems in Cuba escalated, the *New York Journal* and the *New York World* continued their sensationalistic coverage, the height of which came when the American ship *Maine* blew up in a Cuban harbor. The military cautioned against jumping to conclusions, but both the *Journal* and the *World* placed the blame for

Go On

the explosion on Spain. They called for President William McKinley to declare war. The military eventually determined that the *Maine's* explosion was in fact caused by outside forces, and the United States declared war on Spain on April 25, 1898.

10 Many people feel that without the pressure of the yellow press, the United States would not have entered the war with Spain. Some have gone so far as to call it the "Newspapers' War." While newspapers may have fueled public opinion of the war, they certainly were not solely responsible for the United States government's decision to declare war on Spain. Nonetheless, the Cuban Revolution, the Spanish-American War, and yellow journalism will forever share a historical link, as will Hearst and Pulitzer.

1 What is the **best** meaning of *dubbed* as it is used in paragraph 5?

A changed

B termed

C adapted

D expanded

2 According to the article, what was the main reason people enjoyed reading Hearst's and Pulitzer's newspapers?

A They were eloquent.

B They were inexpensive.

C They were thrilling.

D They were colorful.

3 How did Hearst prove that Pulitzer stole news from the pages of his newspaper?

A He hired away Pulitzer's entire staff of reporters and illustrators.

B He sent a reporter to capture Pulitzer in the act of stealing a story.

C He discovered a telegram between Pulitzer and one of his reporters.

D He planted a fake story, which Pulitzer copied the next day.

4 Which of the following is **most likely** the purpose of the article?

A to entertain readers with a story about successful newspaper owners

B to inform readers about a form of journalism that relied on sensationalism

C to convince readers that journalists were responsible for starting a war

D to persuade readers to read newspapers on a regular basis

Go On

5 Which newspaper did Hearst purchase after he acquired the *San Francisco Examiner*?

A   *New York World*

B   *New York Journal*

C   *San Francisco Enquirer*

D   *New York Times*

6 According to the article, which of the following would **most likely** be published in a tabloid?

A   a profile of a local mayor

B   a story about the beauty of winter

C   a story about a cow with two heads

D   an article about a house fire

7 Based on the article, which of the following **best** describes Hearst's approach to selling newspapers?

A   modest

B   original

C   dishonest

D   indifferent

8 According to the article, who was responsible for the explosion of the American ship *Maine*?

A   Pulitzer

B   Spain

C   Cuba

D   Hearst

Go On

Write your answer to open-response question 9 in the space provided on your Answer Sheet.

9   Describe how Pulitzer was caught stealing news from another newspaper. Use relevant and specific information from the article to support your answer.

In this excerpt from the Greek drama Antigone, *Polyneices and Eteocles, two brothers on opposite sides of a civil war in Thebes, have been killed in battle. Creon, Thebes's new ruler, has announced that while the body of Eteocles will be honored with a proper burial, Polyneices's body will lay unburied. In this excerpt, his sisters, Antigone and Ismene, discuss what action should be taken. Read the excerpt and use the information to answer the questions that follow.*

Excerpt from Antigone

by **Sophocles**

1   ANTIGONE: Ismene, sister, mine own dear sister, knowest thou what ill there is, of all bequeathed by Oedipus, that Zeus fulfils not for us twain while we live? Nothing painful is there, nothing fraught with ruin, no shame, no dishonour, that I have not seen in thy woes and mine. And now what new edict is this of which they tell, that our Captain hath just published to all Thebes? Knowest thou aught? Hast thou heard? Or is it hidden from thee that our friends are threatened with the doom of our foes?

ISMENE: No word of friends, Antigone, gladsome or painful, hath come to me, since we two sisters were bereft of brothers twain, killed in one day by twofold blow; and since in this last night the Argive host hath fled, know no more, whether my fortune be brighter, or more grievous.

ANTIGONE: I knew it well, and therefore sought to bring thee beyond the gates of the court, that thou mightest hear alone.

ISMENE: What is it? 'Tis plain that thou art brooding on some dark tidings.

5   ANTIGONE: What, hath not Creon destined our brothers, the one to honoured burial, the other to un-buried shame? Eteocles, they say, with due observance of right and custom, he hath laid in the earth, for his honour among the dead below. But the hapless corpse of Polyneices—as rumour saith, it hath been published to the town that none shall entomb him or mourn, but leave unwept, unsepulchred, a welcome store for the birds, as they espy him, to feast on at will. Such, 'tis said, is the edict that the good Creon hath set forth for thee and for me,—yes, for me,—and is coming hither to proclaim it clearly to those who know it not; nor counts the matter light, but, whoso disobeys in aught, his doom is death by stoning before all the folk. Thou knowest it now; and thou wilt soon show whether thou art nobly bred, or the base daughter of a noble line.

ISMENE: Poor sister,-and if things stand thus, what could I help to do or undo?

ANTIGONE: Consider if thou wilt share the toil and the deed.

ISMENE: In what venture? What can be thy meaning?

ANTIGONE: Wilt thou aid this hand to lift the dead?

10 ISMENE: Thou wouldst bury him,—when 'tis forbidden to Thebes?

ANTIGONE: I will do my part,—and thine, if thou wilt not,—to a brother. False to him will I never be found.

ISMENE: Ah, over-bold! when Creon hath forbidden?

ANTIGONE: Nay, he hath no right to keep me from mine own.

Go On

10 Read these lines from the play.

> I will do my part,—and thine, if thou
> wilt not,—to a brother.

What does Antigone mean in this line?

A She will ask for help burying her brother.

B She will bury her brother on her own.

C She will take responsibility for her actions.

D She will listen to Creon without question.

11 What does Ismene mean when she says, " 'Tis plain that thou art brooding on some dark tidings"?

A She knows her sister plans on going out at night.

B She thinks her sister is thinking about something bad.

C She knows her sister is remembering the past.

D She thinks her sister feels badly about something.

12 According to the excerpt, which of these would **best** describe Antigone?

A considerate

B persuasive

C responsible

D defiant

13 What does the word *toil* mean in line 7?

A act

B pain

C work

D blame

Go On

In his poem "The Tidings," nineteenth-century Irish poet and translator Denis Florence MacCarthy expresses his feelings for the arrival of spring. Read this excerpt from the poem and answer the questions that follow.

An Excerpt from
"The Tidings"

by **Denis Florence MacCarthy**

1   A bright beam came to my window frame,
     This sweet May morn,
     And it said to the cold, hard glass:
     Oh! let me pass,
5   For I have good news to tell,
     The queen of the dewy dell,[1]
     The beautiful May is born!

     Warm with the race, through the open space,
     This sweet May morn,
10   Came a soft wind out of the skies:
     And it said to my heart—Arise!
     Go forth from the winter's fire,
     For the child of thy long desire,
     The beautiful May is born!

15   The bright beam glanced and the soft wind danced,
     This sweet May morn,
     Over my cheek and over my eyes;
     And I said with a glad surprise:
     Oh! lead me forth, ye blessed twain,[2]
20   Over the hill and over the plain,
     Where the beautiful May is born.

     Through the open door leaped the beam before
     This sweet May morn,
     And the soft wind floated along,
25   Like a poet's song,
     Warm from his heart and fresh from his brain;
     And they led me over the mount and plain,
     To the beautiful May new-born.

Go On

My guide so bright and my guide so light,
30 This sweet May morn,
Led me along o'er the grassy ground,
And I knew by each joyous sight and sound,
The fields so green and the skies so gay,
That heaven and earth kept holiday,
35 That the beautiful May was born.

Out of the sea with their eyes of glee,
This sweet May morn,
Came the blue waves hastily on;
And they murmuring cried—Thou happy one!
40 Show us, O Earth! thy darling child,
For we heard far out on the ocean wild,
That the beautiful May was born. . . .

Under the eaves and through the leaves
This sweet May morn,
45 The soft wind whispering flew:
And it said to the listening birds—Oh, you,
Sweet choristers of the skies,
Awaken your tenderest lullabies,
For the beautiful May now born.

50 The white cloud flew to the uttermost blue,
This sweet May morn,
It bore, like a gentle carrier-dove,
The blessed news to the realms above;
While its sister coo'd[3] in the midst of the grove,
55 And within my heart the spirit of love,
That the beautiful May was born!

---

1. *Dell* = valley
2. *Twain* = two things
3. *Coo'd* = to made the sound of a dove

Go On

14 What metaphor does the speaker use for May in the poem?

A a child

B a dove

C the wind

D a love

15 In line 25, what does the simile "Like a poet's song" suggest?

A The wind is beautiful.

B The wind is musical.

C The wind is heartfelt.

D The wind is gentle.

16 What is the effect of the repetition of lines 7 and 14?

A It shows the importance of the subject of the poem.

B It expresses curiosity about the month of May.

C It foreshadows what may come next in the poem.

D It reminds readers of the subject of the poem.

17 In line 47, what does the word *choristers* mean?

A ears

B breezes

C singers

D clouds

Go On

Write your answer to open-response question 18 in the space provided on your Answer Sheet.

18 Describe the tone of "The Tidings," and explain how the author achieves that tone. Use relevant and specific information from the poem to support your answer.

Go On

LANGUAGE AND LITERATURE: SESSION 2

This session contains a reading selection with eight multiple-choice questions and one open-response question. Mark your answers to these questions in the spaces provided on your Answer Sheet.

"A Wagner Matinee" was written by twentieth-century novelist Willa Cather. In this story, narrator Clark Hamilton has moved to Boston and left behind all traces of rural Nebraska, where he was raised with his aunt and uncle. When his aunt comes to visit him in the city, he takes her to a matinee, and she hears music for the first time in many years. Read the story and answer the questions that follow.

An Excerpt from "A Wagner Matinee"

by **Willa Cather**

1 I received one morning a letter, written in pale ink on glassy, blue-lined notepaper, and bearing the post-mark of a little Nebraska village. This communication . . . was from my Uncle Howard and informed me that his wife had been left a small legacy by a bachelor relative who had recently died. . . . It would be necessary for her to go to Boston to attend to the settling of the estate. He requested me to meet her at the station and render her whatever services might be necessary. . . .

2   When the train arrived I had some difficulty in finding my aunt. She was the last of the passengers to alight, and it was not until I got her into the carriage that she seemed really to recognize me. She had come all the way in a day coach; her linen duster had become black with soot, and her black bonnet gray with dust, during the journey. . . .

3   My Aunt Georgiana had been a music teacher at the Boston Conservatory, somewhere back in the latter sixties. One summer, while visiting in the little village among the Green Mountains where her ancestors had dwelt for generations, she had kindled the callow fancy of the most idle and shiftless of all the village lads. . . . The upshot of this inexplicable infatuation was that she eloped with him, eluding the reproaches of her family and the criticisms of her friends by going with him to the Nebraska frontier. Carpenter, who, of course, had no money, had taken a homestead in Red Willow County, fifty miles from the railroad. . . . For thirty years my aunt had not been further than fifty miles from the homestead. . . .

4   I owed to this woman most of the good that ever came my way in my boyhood, and had a reverential affection for her. During the years when I was riding herd for my uncle, my aunt, after cooking the three meals . . . would often stand until midnight at her ironing board, with me at the kitchen table beside her, hearing me recite Latin declensions and conjugations, gently shaking me when my drowsy head sank down over a page of irregular verbs. It was to her, at her ironing or mending, that I read my first Shakespeare, and her old textbook on mythology was the first that ever came into my empty hands. She taught me my scales and exercises, too—on the little parlor organ, which her husband had bought her after fifteen years. . . .

5   When my aunt appeared on the morning after her arrival she was still in a semi-somnambulant state. . . . I had planned a little pleasure for her that afternoon, to repay her for some of the glorious moments she had given me when we used to milk together in the straw-thatched cowshed and she, because I was more than usually tired, or because her husband had spoken sharply to me, would tell me of the splendid performance of the *Huguenots* she had seen in Paris, in her youth. At two o'clock the Sym-

Go On

phony Orchestra was to give a Wagner program, and I intended to take my aunt; though, as I conversed with her I grew doubtful about her enjoyment of it. Indeed, for her own sake, I could only wish her taste for such things quite dead, and the long struggle mercifully ended at last. . . . She was chiefly concerned that she had forgotten to leave instructions about feeding half-skimmed milk to a certain weakling calf, "old Maggie's calf, you know, Clark," she explained, evidently having forgotten how long I had been away. . . .

6   I asked her whether she had ever heard any of the Wagnerian operas and found that she had not. . . . I began to think it would have been best to get her back to Red Willow County without waking her, and regretted having suggested the concert.

7   From the time we entered the concert hall, however, she was a trifle less passive and inert, and for the first time seemed to perceive her surroundings. I had felt some trepidation lest she might become aware of the absurdities of her attire, or might experience some painful embarrassment at stepping suddenly into the world to which she had been dead for a quarter of a century. . . .

8   When the musicians came out and took their places, she gave a little stir of anticipation and looked with quickening interest down over the rail at that invariable grouping, perhaps the first wholly familiar thing that had greeted her eye since she had left old Maggie and her weakling calf. I could feel how all those details sank into her soul, for I had not forgotten how they had sunk into mine when I came fresh from plowing forever and forever between green aisles of corn, where, as in a treadmill, one might walk from daybreak to dusk without perceiving a shadow of change. I recalled how, in the first orchestra I had ever heard, those long bow strokes seemed to draw the heart out of me. . . .

9   When the horns drew out the first strain of the Pilgrim's chorus my Aunt Georgiana clutched my coat sleeve. Then it was I first realized that for her this broke a silence of thirty years; the inconceivable silence of the plains. . . .

10   The overture closed; my aunt released my coat sleeve, but she said nothing. . . . What, I wondered, did she get from it? She had often told me of Mozart's operas and Meyerbeer's, and I could remember hearing her sing, years ago, certain melodies of Verdi's. When I had fallen ill with a fever in her house she used to sit by my cot in the evening—when the cool, night wind blew in through the faded mosquito netting tacked over the window, and I lay watching a certain bright star that burned red above the corn-field—and sing "Home to our mountains, O, let us return!" in a way fit to break the heart of a Vermont boy near dead of homesickness already.

11   I watched her closely through the prelude to *Tristan and Isolde* . . . but she sat mutely staring at the violin bows that drove obliquely downward, like the pelting streaks of rain in a summer shower. Had this music any message for her?

12   . . . Soon after the tenor began the "Prize Song," I heard a quick drawn breath and turned to my aunt. Her eyes were closed, but the tears were glistening on her cheeks, and I think, in a moment more, they were in my eyes as well. It never really died, then—the soul that can suffer so excruciatingly and so interminably; it withers to the outward eye only; like that strange moss which can lie on a dusty shelf half a century and yet, if placed in water, grows green again. . . .

13   Her lip quivered and she hastily put her handkerchief up to her mouth. From behind it she murmured, "And you have been hearing this ever since you left me, Clark?" Her question was the gentlest and saddest of reproaches.

14   My aunt wept quietly, but almost continuously, as a shallow vessel overflows in a rainstorm. From time to time her dim eyes looked up at the lights which studded the ceiling, burning softly under their dull glass globes; doubtless they were stars in truth to her. I was still perplexed as to what measure of musical comprehension was left to her, she who had heard nothing but the singing of gospel hymns at

Methodist services in the square frame schoolhouse on Section Thirteen for so many years. I was wholly unable to gauge how much of it had been dissolved in soapsuds, or worked into bread, or milked into the bottom of a pail.

15   The concert was over; the people filed out of the hall chattering and laughing, glad to relax and find the living level again, but my kinswoman made no effort to rise. The harpist slipped its green felt cover over his instrument; the flute players shook the water from their mouthpieces; the men of the orchestra went out one by one, leaving the stage to the chairs and music stands, empty as a winter cornfield.

16   I spoke to my aunt. She burst into tears and sobbed pleadingly. "I don't want to go, Clark, I don't want to go!"

17   I understood. For her, just outside the door of the concert hall, lay the black pond with the cattle-tracked bluffs; the tall, unpainted house, with weather-curled boards; naked as a tower, the crook-backed ash seedlings where the dishcloths hung to dry; the gaunt, molting turkeys picking up refuse about the kitchen door.

19   Read this sentence from paragraph 3.

> One summer, while visiting in the little village among the Green Mountains where her ancestors had dwelt for generations, she had kindled the callow fancy of the most idle and shiftless of all the village lads.

What is the author implying?

A   A lazy boy with no prospects was attracted to her.

B   Many people were inspired by her.

C   She dressed very beautifully.

D   She was very social.

20   Which of the following **best** describes the tone of the story?

A   reflective

B   objective

C   humorous

D   resentful

21   In the story, when the narrator is at home, she spends most of her time doing what?

A   listening to music

B   doing chores

C   reading Shakespeare

D   taking care of her husband

22   What does Aunt Georgiana realize in the story?

A   She truly misses her life on the farm.

B   She has greatly missed listening to music.

C   She has lost the love of her nephew.

D   She wants to play piano again.

Go On

23 What quality of the music is **most** surprising to the narrator's aunt?

A the tempo

B the volume

C the beauty

D the style

24 Which word **best** describes Aunt Georgiana in paragraph 16?

A confused

B shocked

C sentimental

D regretful

25 What part of speech is the word *hastily* in paragraph 13?

A verb

B noun

C adjective

D adverb

26 Why does the narrator regret having suggested the concert to his aunt?

A She seems very tired and needs to sleep.

B She is in a hurry to return to the farm.

C She seems to have forgotten such things.

D She may feel out of place because of her clothing.

Go On

Write your answer to open-response question 27 in the space provided on your Answer Sheet.

 27 In this story, how is life in Boston different from where Aunt Georgiana lives? Use relevant and specific information from the story to support your answer.

LANGUAGE AND LITERATURE: SESSION 3

This session contains two reading selections with twelve multiple-choice questions and one open-response question. Mark your answers to these questions in the spaces provided on your Answer Sheet.

In "Daydreams Save the Day," Ricardo Sanchez discusses instances when daydreaming can help people. Read the article and answer the questions that follow.

Daydreams Save the Day

by **Ricardo Sanchez**

1   Many students have gotten in trouble for daydreaming in class. It's not a good idea to be thinking about your new skateboard or your weekend plans when you should be learning algebra! It is rude to the instructor, and you might not learn what you need to know. However, many scientists agree that daydreaming itself is not a bad thing at all. In fact, daydreams can make your life happier and healthier in numerous ways.

2   Some psychologists believe that the average person daydreams for many hours each day. Critics of daydreaming say that this is a dreadful waste of time. Daydreaming usually does not result in any obvious progress; it is usually seen as something that keeps people from making progress. This is not really the case, however. Sometimes daydreaming can help people sort out their minds and get their ideas in order so they can think and behave a lot more effectively. Their daydreams can make them more productive workers or students and make future progress easier.

3   Among the many negative stereotypes surrounding daydreamers is that they are lazy and shirk responsibilities. While this can be true, it definitely is not always true. Sometimes daydreams actually give people a goal to work toward. For instance, a writer might daydream about seeing his or her book in print, and this image builds determination to keep on writing. In this way, daydreams can be a method of visualizing success in the future. Some athletes use "positive thinking" visualization while practicing. By thinking about their challenges and imagining success in the end, they tend to perform much better than athletes who have not prepared their minds.

4   A third criticism of daydreams is that too much daydreaming can make people unhappy. Of course, if a person daydreams *all day*, he or she will probably lose track of the events of real life! He or she might start to "live in the past" or in some unrealistic dream world. But for people who do a regular amount of daydreaming, the practice can make them happier. This can happen in many ways.

5   For one, daydreaming allows the mind to relax. Especially in stressful times, giving your mind a break is a great idea. Taking a "mini-vacation" by daydreaming can make a person's brain feel energized and refreshed. These vacations are also great for overcoming boredom. Excessive boredom can have negative effects on people and cause them to feel gloomy and tired. A little daydreaming here and there can relieve the nasty effects of boredom.

Go On

6   Many psychologists think that daydreams can also help remove fear and conflict from our lives. Just like athletes who use daydreams to prepare for events, other people can use them to learn to deal with themselves and others. If two people aren't getting along, they might be able to daydream, or visualize, ways in which they could reconcile. They might even be able to use daydreams to imagine the others' points of view and find similarities or shared interests between themselves and others. Daydreaming can help us expand our minds, and that helps us find new ways to get along with others.

7   In much the same way, people can use daydreams to ease, and even conquer, their fears. For example, if a person has a powerful fear, or phobia, of heights, he or she might imagine safely climbing higher and higher on a hill. This can prepare the person to remain calm while climbing the hill. "Positive thinking" daydreams can strengthen a person's courage considerably. Many people have used this simple technique to conquer their phobias.

8   Many good kinds of daydreaming help people improve their lives. However, bad types of daydreaming exist as well. One of these is "negative daydreaming," which occurs most frequently in the behavior we know as "worrying." Some people get caught up in worries, and spend their days nervously picturing all sorts of frightening and embarrassing events. Worries can have a terrible effect on people's lives. Sometimes worries can keep people awake all night; other times worries and stress can weaken the body, causing people to get sick more easily.

9   One of the best ways to combat negative daydreams like worrying is to counter them with "positive daydreams." Instead of worrying, a person can take a more relaxed look at his or her concerns. He or she can reflect on the past, imagine some possibilities of the future, and then try to decide how to handle worries. By using positive daydreams and visualizations, you may well be able to overcome many kinds of negative thoughts and feelings.

10   Daydreams play an important role in our daily lives, a role that not many people stop to consider. Good daydreams can make us healthy and happy, and bad daydreams can do just the opposite. But just remember—no daydreams are good daydreams in algebra class!

---

28 According to the article, which of these is an example of negative daydreaming?

A visualizing the completion of a project before it is finished

B allowing your mind to wander for a few minutes

C thinking about conquering a fear

D losing track of real life while thinking about the past

29 Which of the following is **closest** in meaning to the word *shirk* as it is used in paragraph 3?

A replace

B juggle

C accept

D avoid

Go On

30 What is the author's purpose in writing this article?

A to entertain readers with stories of people who daydream often

B to convince readers that daydreaming is more than a waste of time

C to teach readers how to analyze their own daydreams

D to explain the difference between positive and negative daydreaming

31 What is this article **mainly** about?

A how excessive daydreaming can make people unhappy

B why daydreaming should never happen in algebra class

C why daydreaming is sometimes a good thing

D how daydreaming can help people from being bored

32 According to the article, how are daydreams about conflicts helpful?

A They help to stop us from feeling gloomy and tired.

B Athletes use daydreaming to prepare for events.

C They can help us understand other people's feelings.

D They have been shown to help people get over their fears.

33 In paragraph 6, what does the word *reconcile* mean?

A to settle a conflict

B to make consistent

C to submit to something unpleasant

D to double-check for accuracy

34 In the article, why does the author put several words in quotation marks?

A to show that they are often misunderstood

B to show that they are quoted from a source

C to emphasize their importance

D to indicate psychological terminology

35 According to the article, during which time would daydreaming be **most** helpful?

A when remembering the past

B when feeling sad

C when working toward a goal

D when concentrating in class

Go On

Write your answer to open-response question 36 in the space provided on your Answer Sheet.

 Explain how daydreaming can help someone conquer a fear. Use relevant and specific information from the article to support your answer.

Go On

Charlotte Perkins Gilman was a feminist author during the late 1800s and early 1900s. While the "Yellow Wallpaper" is fictional, it is based on Gilman's experience of being diagnosed as a hysteric and suffering confinement as a cure. Read the excerpt and answer the questions that follow.

Excerpt from "The Yellow Wallpaper"

by **Charlotte Perkins Gilman**

1   We have been here two weeks, and I haven't felt like writing before, since that first day. I am sitting by the window now, up in this atrocious nursery, and there is nothing to hinder my writing as much as I please, save lack of strength.

2   John is away all day, and even some nights when his cases are serious. I am glad my case is not serious! But these nervous troubles are dreadfully depressing. John does not know how much I really suffer. He knows there is no REASON to suffer, and that satisfies him.

3   Of course it is only nervousness. It does weigh on me so not to do my duty in any way! I meant to be such a help to John, such a real rest and comfort, and here I am a comparative burden already!

4   Nobody would believe what an effort it is to do what little I am able,—to dress and entertain, and other things. It is fortunate Mary is so good with the baby. Such a dear baby! And yet I CANNOT be with him, it makes me so nervous.

5   I suppose John never was nervous in his life. He laughs at me so about this wall-paper! At first he meant to repaper the room, but afterwards he said that I was letting it get the better of me, and that nothing was worse for a nervous patient than to give way to such fancies.

6   He said that after the wall-paper was changed it would be the heavy bedstead, and then the barred windows, and then that gate at the head of the stairs, and so on. "You know the place is doing you good," he said, "and really, dear, I don't care to renovate the house just for a three months' rental."

7   "Then do let us go downstairs," I said, "there are such pretty rooms there." Then he took me in his arms and called me a blessed little goose, and said he would go down to the cellar, if I wished, and have it whitewashed into the bargain.

8   But he is right enough about the beds and windows and things. It is an airy and comfortable room as any one need wish, and, of course, I would not be so silly as to make him uncomfortable just for a whim. I'm really getting quite fond of the big room, all but that horrid paper. . . .

9   Out of one window I can see the garden, those mysterious deep-shaded arbors, the riotous old-fashioned flowers, and bushes and gnarly trees. Out of another I get a lovely view of the bay and a little private wharf belonging to the estate. There is a beautiful shaded lane that runs down there from the house. I always fancy I see people walking in these numerous paths and arbors, but John has cautioned me not to give way to fancy in the least. He says that with my imaginative power and habit of story-making, a nervous weakness like mine is sure to lead to all manner of excited fancies, and that I ought to use my will and good sense to check the tendency. So I try.

10   I think sometimes that if I were only well enough to write a little it would relieve the press of ideas and rest me. But I find I get pretty tired when I try. It is so discouraging not to have any advice and companionship about my work. When I get really well, John says we will ask Cousin Henry and Julia down for a long visit; but he says he would as soon put fireworks in my pillow-case as to let me have those stimulating people about now. I wish I could get well faster. But I must not think about that. This paper looks to me as if it KNEW what a vicious influence it had!

Go On

11   There is a recurrent spot where the pattern lolls like a broken neck and two bulbous eyes stare at you upside down. I get positively angry with the impertinence of it and the everlastingness. Up and down and sideways they crawl, and those absurd, unblinking eyes are everywhere. There is one place where two breadths didn't match, and the eyes go all up and down the line, one a little higher than the other. I never saw so much expression in an inanimate thing before, and we all know how much expression they have! I used to lie awake as a child and get more entertainment and terror out of blank walls and plain furniture than most children could find in a toy store. . . .

12   The wall-paper, as I said before, is torn off in spots, and it sticketh closer than a brother—they must have had perseverance as well as hatred. Then the floor is scratched and gouged and splintered, the plaster itself is dug out here and there, and this great heavy bed which is all we found in the room, looks as if it had been through the wars. But I don't mind it a bit—only the paper.

37 In the excerpt, why does the author put several words in capital letters?

  A to reveal the speaker's feelings about not being able to write

  B to explain the damage the room upstairs has endured

  C to describe John's feelings about the wallpaper

  D to emphasize the speaker's frustration with her situation

38 What does the author **most likely** mean when she writes that the wallpaper "sticketh closer than a brother" in paragraph 12?

  A The wallpaper has become important to her.

  B The wallpaper is always on her mind.

  C The wallpaper reminds her of her brother.

  D The wallpaper is physically close to her.

39 Which word **best** describes the narrator's tone in paragraph 5?

  A respectful

  B excited

  C surprised

  D spiteful

40 According to the excerpt, why won't John change the wallpaper?

  A He is too busy working.

  B He thinks it will make her nervous.

  C The rest of the room is very nice.

  D She will only be there for a short time.

Stop

ANSWERS

Composition

WRITING PROMPT SAMPLE ANSWER

In the play *A Raisin in the Sun*, Walter Younger makes a bad decision that affects his entire family. The Youngers are an African American family living in the South Side of Chicago in the 1950s. After the death of Walter's father, the Younger family receives ten-thousand dollars from Mr. Younger's life insurance policy. All the family members have different ideas about how the money should be spent. Mrs. Younger wants to move out of the family's apartment and buy a house. Walter wants to invest in a liquor store business with his friends. Walter's sister, Beneatha, thinks that they should use the money to send her to medical school.

Everyone in the family believes that his or her idea for the money is the best, but Walter's plans ultimately cost the family everything. After his mother uses some of the money for the down payment on a house, Walter's friend, Willy, convinces him to invest the rest of the money in a new liquor store. Walter gives Willy the money and is horrified when Willy runs off with it. Walter believed that the liquor store would end the family's financial problems forever, but now they are in more trouble than they were before.

The family is moving to a new house that they may no longer be able to afford because they have lost the money. Walter's hasty decision makes the family's future uncertain. If he had kept the money, his family's financial situation would not be unstable and there would be far less tension and strain between Walter's already stressed family members.

LANGUAGE AND LITERATURE

1   B   Standard 4

When other newspapers dubbed Hearst and Pulitzer's style of reporting "yellow journalism," they called or termed it that.

2   C   Standard 8

The article mentions several times that people loved these newspapers because they were exciting.

3   D   Standard 8

Hearst proved that Pulitzer stole stories by printing a fake story in the *New York Journal* that appeared in Pulitzer's newspaper, the *New York World*, the next day.

4   B   Standard 13

The article does not convince or persuade. While it does entertain, this is not its main purpose.

5   B   Standard 8

Wanting to own a paper in New York, Hearst purchased the *New York Journal* after he acquired the *San Francisco Examiner*.

6   C   Standard 8

Tabloids, such as those discussed in the article, publish stories that are embellished or made up. They strive to be sensational.

7   C   Standard 12

Hearst worked with Pulitzer, so his style was not original. It was, however, dishonest.

8   B   Standard 8

The article says that Spain was responsible for the explosion of the ship *Maine*.

9   Sample answer   Standard 8

Pulitzer was caught stealing news from another newspaper when Hearst placed a fabricated story in his paper about the death of Colonel Reflipe W. Thenuz. The next day, details of this fictional colonel's death were reprinted in Pulitzer's paper.

10   B   Standard 15

Antigone means that she will bury him on her own out of respect.

11 B Standard 15

Ismene knows that Antigone is planning to do something that is against Creon's orders.

12 D Standard 12

While Antigone is *considerate* of her brother's honor, *defiant* is a better answer choice because she is openly defying Creon's orders.

13 C Standard 4

The word *toil* means *to labor* or *work*.

14 A Standard 14

The speaker of the poem refers to a child many times, such as when he says "the beautiful May was born."

15 D Standard 14

The line above this one offers a clue: the speaker says the soft wind floated along like a poet's song.

16 A Standard 14

The speaker is thrilled about spring, the subject of the poem. Repeating this line emphasizes the importance of spring to the speaker.

17 C Standard 4

The choristers are singers. The speaker is referring to the birds singing in the skies. The word *lullabies* in the following line also offers a clue.

18 Sample answer Standard 14

The tone of "The Tidings" is very exciting. The author is thrilled that it is May and spring. He achieves this tone by carefully choosing words and punctuation. He uses descriptive words such as *whispering* and *tenderest*. He calls May "Thou happy one!" and a "darling child."

19 A Standard 8

The author means that of all the boys in the village she could have attracted, the one who most admired her was the laziest one.

20 A Standard 15

Throughout most of the story, the narrator reflects on his aunt's life and what she lost by living in the country.

21   B   Standard 8

The answer to this question is right in the story. The narrator says that he could not tell how much of his aunt's love of music had been "dissolved in soapsuds, or worked into bread, or milked into the bottom of a pail."

22   B   Standard 11

The major theme in this story is that hearing the music at the matinee made Aunt Georgiana realize how much she had been missing music, which she loved.

23   C   Standard 8

The beauty of the music is most surprising to Aunt Georgiana.

24   D   Standard 12

Aunt Georgiana is not really confused in this paragraph; she is regretful and does not want to go back to the farm.

25   D   Standard 4

Hastily is an adverb. In paragraph 13, it modifies the verb *put*.

26   C   Standard 11

The narrator says that he regretted suggesting the concert to his aunt because she is so preoccupied with the farm that she seems to have forgotten her love of music.

27   Sample answer   Standard 11

Life in Boston sharply contrasts with the life Aunt Georgiana has grown accustomed to. She has little money in the country, and the narrator mentions her spending a great deal of time ironing and mending clothes. She worries about a weak calf, and her clothes are dirty because she traveled there in a day coach.

Life is busy in Boston and, unlike the country, there are many people who seem to be occupied with jobs that do not require manual labor. The narrator implies that the concert hall is filled with beautifully dressed people, and he worries that his aunt's country attire will look absurd in comparison.

28   D   Standard 8

The only answer that is definitely negative is answer choice D.

29   D   Standard 4

If you *shirk* responsibilities, you avoid them.

30 D Standard 13

The author is not trying to convince or entertain and he does not teach readers how to analyze their own daydreams. Answer choice D is the best answer.

31 C Standard 8

The author mainly discusses the positive aspects of daydreaming.

32 C Standard 8

The part of the article that discusses how daydreaming can help us resolve conflicts mentions that thinking about the other person might help us resolve the conflict.

33 A Standard 4

If you *reconcile* a conflict, you settle or solve it.

34 D Standard 5

The author puts words in quotation marks that relate to psychology. He does this because these words are psychological terms and might not be clear to the reader.

35 C Standard 8

The answer to this question is right in the passage. The author says that daydreaming is helpful when working toward a goal. He notes that if you picture yourself reaching that goal, you are more likely to reach it.

36 Sample answer   Standard 8

In paragraph 7, the article explains that daydreaming can help ease or even conquer a person's fears. If a person imagines him- or herself doing the activity that he or she is afraid of, it can prepare the person to remain calm while performing the activity in real life. The article says that "positive thinking" daydreams can make a person more courageous.

37 D Standard 5

The author puts words in capital letters to emphasize them and show that the speaker is extremely frustrated.

38 B Standard 15

The wallpaper may not be physically close to the narrator, but she cannot stop looking at it and thinking about it. Answer choice B is the best answer.

39 D Standard 5

The narrator seems bitter or spiteful when she says, "I suppose John was never nervous in his life." Then she explains that John laughs at her.

40 D Standard 11

At first John says that he will change the wallpaper, but then he says it seems a waste of time because they will only be there for three months.

MCAS Grade 10, English Language Arts

Practice Test 2

Composition

WRITING PROMPT

Often in works of literature, one character is the complete opposite of another character. From a work of literature you have read in or out of school, select two characters that are complete opposites of one another. In a well-developed composition, identify both characters, describe what makes them opposites, and explain why their differences are important to the work of literature.

LANGUAGE AND LITERATURE: SESSION 1

This session contains two reading selections with eleven multiple-choice questions and two open-response questions. Mark your answers to these questions in the spaces provided on your Answer Sheet.

This article describes the discovery of a shipwreck that was buried on land. Read "Buried Boats" and answer the questions that follow.

Buried Boats

1   When most people think of a shipwreck, they imagine the remains of a huge wooden or metal boat crashed along the bottom of the ocean. Fish swim in and out of the mangled boat's hull, and coral and seaweed cling to its sides. Meanwhile, divers with scuba gear and cameras paddle their way into the depths to explore inside the long-forgotten vessel. They might find anything from old pottery to rusty cannons to pirate gold, but one thing is for certain: the deep, cold water has swallowed up the ship and kept it secret for a very long time.

2   Surprisingly, though, water is not always a necessary element in shipwreck explorations. Few people realize that many important shipwrecks can be found *on land*. Trading skiffs, warships, and pirate galleons alike have been found buried deep in riverbeds, hilltops, and cornfields throughout the world.

3   The seemingly unlikely event of a boat being buried is actually fairly common. Millions of boats travel various parts of this world, accessing thousands of bodies of water in the process. That means there are numerous opportunities for ships to sink, and, indeed, ships do sink on a regular basis. Let's say a ship is traveling down a river and it springs a leak, founders, strikes the bottom of the river, and sinks into the mud. Over subsequent years, more mud and sediment might build up on top of the shipwreck, partially or wholly concealing it.

4   The next step in this process is more unlikely but not uncommon. The river may change its course by covering a new section of land or beginning to flow in a different direction. Many things can cause a river to change its course, including damming, erosion, and floods.

5   After the river has moved, its old riverbed (where the shipwreck still lies) is uncovered. Former riverbeds have rich, moist soil and make excellent farmlands. If a farmer finds such soil and plants there, the crops will likely grow well. Within a short time, the land will permanently lose any familiarity to a riverbed; a casual observer would not realize that a river ever used to traverse it. An observer would certainly never dream that there might be a shipwreck buried beneath it.

6   In 1988, brothers David and Greg Hawley found the wreck of a steamboat that sank on September 5, 1856—and they found it buried forty-five feet below the ground in the middle of a farmer's cornfield!

7   The Hawleys learned about the steamboat, named the *Arabia*, while reading an old newspaper. According to the article, the ship sank in a river a mile below a town called Parkville. The brothers were puzzled; they could find Parkville on a modern map, but there was no river anywhere near it. How could there conceivably be a ship there?

Go On

8   David Hawley found an old map of the town, and it was immediately evident to him that a river had once flowed near Parkville. So they decided to compare the old and new maps and figure out what land used to be part of the riverbed. After drawing up a new map, they marked off all the land within a mile of Parkville and then visited some local farmers. After obtaining permission, the Hawleys went into some cornfields with metal detectors. They weren't detecting for old coins or jewelry; they were searching for a shipwreck.

9   It didn't take long before the brothers' metal detectors located the huge metal boilers and engines of the old steamship. Caught up in the thrill of discovery, the Hawleys and some friends gathered some money and launched into a massive effort to excavate the deep-down artifact. The project ended up being costly and time-consuming, but the diggers were determined to bring this piece of history back to the surface.

10   It wasn't as easy as scooping up sand with a shovel. To the Hawleys' dismay, they found that the field was solid, but there was plenty of water underneath. As they dug into the sandy soil, they found a miniature river of muddy water coursing beneath. Undeterred, they built twenty irrigation wells and constructed water pumps nearby to drain water from the excavation site. They had to work fast, too—if they did not find the ship by spring, heavy rains might arrive and wash away all their efforts.

11   After almost five months of strenuous labor, the brothers and their helpers finally sighted the superstructure of the *Arabia*. Although it was filled with mud, they were eventually able to clean it out and explore inside. They were the first people to set foot in the boat in more than a hundred years, and the items they found had not seen sunlight in just as long.

12   The *Arabia* was an invaluable time capsule, containing everything from unopened passengers' suitcases to jars of blueberry pie filling, all well preserved by the mud. The searchers also found crates of Asian silk, British dishes, South American tobacco, and French perfume. There was no doubt that the Arabia was a well-stocked trading ship.

13   Examining the long-lost ship also exposed clues to its demise. The Hawleys learned that the Arabia was carrying hundreds of tons of freight and passengers when it struck a submerged tree. The tree, like a spear, ripped open the ship and sent it foundering toward the riverbed. Although the passengers escaped unharmed, the freight, and the ship itself, fell quickly into the mud. (The *Arabia* was not the only ship to sink in the area, either; the researchers believe that hundreds of ships went down, and many are still buried in farmers' fields.)

14   Although the Hawleys had at first hoped to find golden treasures on board the *Arabia*, they quickly realized that all the history they were rescuing *was* treasure. Their hard work was barely begun; their next steps were to save the artifacts from deteriorating. Delicate items like fabrics and foods had been in cold, watery mud for decades; left out of water, they would quickly rot. Every item from the ship had to be carefully stabilized using various techniques, including soaking, freezing, and coating with wax.

15   Next, the Hawleys had to find a place to store the thousands of relics. The team eventually established a museum dedicated to the history of the *Arabia* and its passengers. Over a hundred thousand people visit the museum each year to catch a unique glimpse of the past—a piece of seafaring history found deep in the dirt.

Go On

1 Which of the following is *most likely* the purpose of the article?

A to explain to readers how people discover and uncover buried boats

B to present the history of the *Arabia* and tell the story of how it sank

C to describe the Hawleys' experience and offer information on buried boats

D to persuade readers to investigate their local history to see if any buried boats might be nearby

2 According to the article, what would be the **best** way to find out if a river has changed its course?

A Use a metal detector to find any buried boats in the area.

B Find an old map of the area and see where the river used to run.

C Find out if there have been any major floods in the area in the last century.

D Ask a historian if any dams have been built in recent years.

3 According to the article, buried boats are different from the regular idea of a shipwreck in that they

A often remain undiscovered rivers and the land near them change over time.

B are easily found through the use of metal detectors.

C are often destroyed by the movement of the dirt above them.

D are more common than regular shipwrecks.

4 What did the Hawleys find when they began to dig in the soil?

A water

B rock

C sand

D mud

Go On

Write your answer to open-response question 5 in the space provided on your Answer Sheet.

5 Explain the steps the Hawleys took to preserve the materials they found inside the ship and why these steps were necessary. Use relevant and specific information from the article to support your answer.

6 Which of the following best summarizes paragraph 14?

A The Hawleys had hoped to find golden treasures on board the *Arabia*.

B Finding a place to store the artifacts found on the *Arabia* proved a difficult task.

C The Hawleys were careful to save the artifacts they found on the *Arabia*.

D If the fabric and foods on the *Arabia* were not in mud, they would have rotted.

7 What is this article **mainly** about?

A how two men discovered the *Arabia*

B why some ships are buried on land

C how two men saved artifacts on the *Arabia*

D why some rivers change course over time

8 Based on the article, which of the following **best** describes how the narrator feels about sunken ships?

A concerned

B excited

C indifferent

D suspicious

Go On

Write your answer to open-response question 9 in the space provided on your Answer Sheet.

9 Explain how the Hawleys discovered the *Arabia*. Use relevant and specific information from the article to support your answer.

Go On

Twentieth-century lyric poet Edna St. Vincent Millay was born in Maine in 1892. She was one of the most famous poets of her time. Read her poem "The Spring and the Fall" and answer the questions that follow.

The Spring and the Fall

by **Edna St. Vincent Millay**

1   In the spring of the year, in the spring of the year,
    I walked the road beside my dear.
    The trees were black where the bark was wet.
    I see them yet, in the spring of the year.
5   He broke me a bough of the blossoming peach
    That was out of the way and hard to reach.

    In the fall of the year, in the fall of the year,
    I walked the road beside my dear.
    The rooks went up with a raucous trill.
10 I hear them still, in the fall of the year.
    He laughed at all I dared to praise,
    And broke my heart, in little ways.

    Year be springing or year be falling,
    The bark will drip and the birds be calling.
15 There's much that's fine to see and hear
    In the spring of a year, in the fall of a year.
    'Tis not love's going hurt my days.
    But that it went in little ways.

Go On

10   Read these lines from the poem.

> 'Tis not love's going hurt my days.
> But that it went in little ways.

What idea is conveyed in these lines?

A   She remembers the little things about her love and it causes her pain.

B   It hurts her that she is reminded of her love each spring and fall.

C   The way her relationship ended hurts more than the fact that it ended.

D   She is over her love but is reminded of him every now and then.

11   What is the effect of the repetition in line 1?

A   It emphasizes that the speaker is remembering something painful.

B   It shows that she looks forward to this season each year.

C   It inspires readers' curiosity about upcoming events in the poem.

D   It emphasizes her fondness for her memory of this time of year.

12   What did the speaker's love do in the fall of the year?

A   He went away from her.

B   He laughed at her.

C   He praised her.

D   He picked her a peach.

13   Which of the following **best** describes the mood of this poem?

A   peaceful

B   lighthearted

C   sad

D   bitter

Go On

LANGUAGE AND LITERATURE: SESSION 2

This session contains two reading selections with twelve multiple-choice questions and one open-response question. Mark your answers to these questions in the spaces provided on your Answer Sheet.

O. Henry was the pseudonym for American writer William Sydney Porter (1862–1910), who was known for his clever writings with surprising endings. Read this excerpt from O. Henry's short story "The Rubber Plant's Story" and answer the questions that follow.

Excerpt from "The Rubber Plant's Story"

by O. Henry

1   . . . The first thing I can remember I had only three leaves and belonged to a member of the pony ballet. I was kept in a sunny window, and was generally watered with seltzer and lemon. I had plenty of fun in those days. I got cross-eyed trying to watch the numbers of the automobiles in the street and the dates on the labels inside at the same time.

2   Well, then the angel that was molting for the musical comedy lost his last feather and the company broke up. The ponies trotted away and I was left in the window ownerless. The janitor gave me to a refined comedy team on the eighth floor, and in six weeks I had been set in the window of five different flats. I took on experience and put out two more leaves.

3   Miss Carruthers, of the refined comedy team—did you ever see her cross both feet back of her neck?—gave me to a friend of hers who had made an unfortunate marriage with a man in a store. Consequently I was placed in the window of a furnished room, rent in advance, water two flights up, gas extra after ten o'clock at night. Two of my leaves withered off here. . . .

4   I don't think I ever had so dull a time as I did with this lady. There was never anything amusing going on inside—she was devoted to her husband, and, besides leaning out the window and flirting with the iceman, she never did a thing toward breaking the monotony.

5   When the couple broke up they left me with the rest of their goods at a second-hand store. I was put out in front for sale along with the jobbiest lot you ever heard of being lumped into one bargain. Think of this little cornucopia of wonders, all for $1.89: Henry James's works, six talking machine records, one pair of tennis shoes, two bottles of horse radish, and a rubber plant—that was me!

6   One afternoon a girl came along and stopped to look at me. She had dark hair and eyes, and she looked slim, and sad around the mouth.

7   "Oh, oh!" she says to herself. "I never thought to see one up here."

8   She pulls out a little purse about as thick as one of my leaves and fingers over some small silver in it. Old Koen, always on the lookout, is ready, rubbing his hands. This girl proceeds to turn down Mr. James and the other commodities. Rubber plants or nothing is the burden of her song. And at last Koen and she come together at 39 cents, and away she goes with me in her arms.

Go On

9   She was a nice girl, but not my style. Too quiet and sober looking. Thinks I to myself: "I'll just about land on the fire-escape of a tenement, six stories up. And I'll spend the next six months looking at clothes on the line."

10   But she carried me to a nice little room only three flights up in quite a decent street. And she put me in the window, of course. And then she went to work and cooked dinner for herself. And what do you suppose she had? Bread and tea and a little dab of jam! Nothing else. Not a single lobster, nor so much as one bottle of champagne. The Carruthers comedy team had both every evening, except now and then when they took a notion for pig's knuckle and kraut.

11   After she had finished her dinner my new owner came to the window and leaned down close to my leaves and cried softly to herself for a while. It made me feel funny. I never knew anybody to cry that way over a rubber plant before. Of course, I've seen a few of 'em turn on the tears for what they could get out of it, but she seemed to be crying just for the pure enjoyment of it. She touched my leaves like she loved 'em, and she bent down her head and kissed each one of 'em. I guess I'm about the toughest specimen of a peripatetic orchid on earth, but I tell you it made me feel sort of queer. Home never was like that to me before. Generally I used to get chewed by poodles and have shirt-waists hung on me to dry, and get watered with coffee grounds and peroxide of hydrogen.

12   This girl had a piano in the room, and she used to disturb it with both hands while she made noises with her mouth for hours at a time. I suppose she was practicing vocal music.

13   One day she seemed very much excited and kept looking at the clock. At eleven somebody knocked and she let in a stout, dark man with tousled black hair. He sat down at once at the piano and played while she sang for him. When she finished she laid one hand on her bosom and looked at him. He shook his head, and she leaned against the piano. "Two years already," she said, speaking slowly—"do you think in two more—or even longer?"

14   The man shook his head again. "You waste your time," he said, roughly I thought. "The voice is not there." And then he looked at her in a peculiar way. "But the voice is not everything," he went on. "You have looks. I can place you, as I told you if—"

15   The girl pointed to the door without saying anything, and the dark man left the room. And then she came over and cried around me again. It's a good thing I had enough rubber in me to be water-proof.

16   About that time somebody else knocked at the door. "Thank goodness," I said to myself. "Here's a chance to get the water-works turned off. I hope it's somebody that's game enough to stand a bird and a bottle to liven things up a little." Tell you the truth, this little girl made me tired. A rubber plant likes to see a little sport now and then. . . .

17   When the girl opens the door in steps a young chap in a traveling cap and picks her up in his arms, and she sings out "Oh, Dick!" and stays there long enough to—well, you've been a rubber plant too, sometimes, I suppose.

18   "Good thing!" says I to myself. "This is livelier than scales and weeping. Now there'll be something doing."

19   "You've got to go back with me," says the young man. "I've come two thousand miles for you. Aren't you tired of it yet. Bess? You've kept all of us waiting so long. Haven't you found out yet what is best?"

20   "The bubble burst only to-day," says the girl. "Come here, Dick, and see what I found the other day on the sidewalk for sale." She brings him by the hand and exhibits yours truly. "How one ever got away up here who can tell? I bought it with almost the last money I had."

21   He looked at me, but he couldn't keep his eyes off her for more than a second. "Do you remember the night, Bess," he said, "when we stood under one of those on the bank of the bayou and what you told me then?"

22   "Geewillikins!" I said to myself. "Both of them stand under a rubber plant! Seems to me they are stretching matters somewhat!"

23   "Do I not," says she, looking up at him and sneaking close to his vest, "and now I say it again, and it is to last forever. Look, Dick, at its leaves, how wet they are. Those are my tears, and it was thinking of you that made them fall."

24   "The dear old magnolias!" says the young man, pinching one of my leaves. "I love them all."

25   Magnolia! Well, wouldn't that—say! those innocents thought I was a magnolia! What the—well, wasn't that tough on a genuine little old New York rubber plant?

14   Which word **best** describes the speaker's tone throughout most of this story?

A angry

B reflective

C attached

D humorous

15   Based on the story, which of the following **best** explains how the narrator feels about the young girl?

A He thinks she is talented and fun.

B He thinks she is sad but interesting.

C He thinks she is boring but decent.

D He thinks she is pretty and exciting.

16   According to the story, what happened to the rubber plant after he lived with a friend of Miss Caruthers?

A He was left with a janitor.

B He was taken to a second-hand store.

C He was put on the fire escape.

D He was left in the window ownerless.

17   What is the meaning of *jobbiest* as it is used in paragraph 5?

A oddest

B prettiest

C largest

D poorest

18   According to the story, what did the rubber plant like about his first owners?

A They put him in a sunny window.

B They were fun to watch.

C They moved him to many places.

D They touched his leaves often.

Go On

19 What does the rubber plant probably mean in paragraph 12 when he says, "This girl had a piano in the room, and she used to disturb it with both hands while she made noises with his mouth for hours at a time"?

A The girl was not very good at making music.

B The girl did not enjoy making music.

C The girl enjoyed practicing music.

D The girl had a strange way of practicing music.

20 What does the rubber plant **probably** mean in paragraph 22 when he says, "Seems to me they are stretching matters somewhat"?

A The couple is overreacting.

B The couple is probably lying.

C The couple is very important.

D The couple is taking too long.

21 According to the story, why did the young girl buy the rubber plant?

A She wanted to give it to Dick.

B It was inexpensive.

C She likes to touch its leaves.

D It looked like a magnolia.

Go On

Write your answer to open-response question 22 in the space provided on your Answer Sheet.

 22 Explain how the rubber plant records the stories of people's lives in this story. Use relevant and specific information form the story to support your answer.

Go On

Thomas Stearns Eliot, better known as T. S. Eliot, was one of the most influential poets of the twentieth century. His poem "The Wasteland" is considered one of the greatest literary achievements of all time. Read this excerpt from the fifth part of "The Wasteland," titled "What the Thunder Said," and answer the questions that follow.

Excerpt from "What the Thunder Said"

by **T. S. Eliot**

1   After the torchlight red on sweaty faces
    After the frosty silence in the gardens
    After the agony in stony places
    The shouting and the crying
5   Prison and palace and reverberation[1]
    Of thunder of spring over distant mountains
    He who was living is now dead
    We who were living are now dying
    With a little patience
10   Here is no water but only rock
    Rock and no water and the sandy road
    The road winding above among the mountains
    Which are mountains of rock without water
    If there were water we should stop and drink
15   Amongst the rock one cannot stop or think
    Sweat is dry and feet are in the sand
    If there were only water amongst the rock
    Dead mountain mouth of carious[2] teeth that cannot spit
    Here one can neither stand not lie nor sit
20   There is not even silence in the mountains
    But dry sterile thunder without rain
    There is not even solitude in the mountains
    But red sullen faces sneer and snarl
    From doors of mudcracked houses

---

1. *Reverberation* = reflection.
2. *Carious* = with cavities.

Go On

23 Which of the following **best** describes the mood of the poem?

A desperate

B thoughtful

C angry

D objective

24 Read these lines from the end of the poem.

> But red sullen faces sneer and snarl
> From doors of mudcracked houses

What does the poet mean in these lines?

A People must stay indoors because of the heat.

B People are poor and bitter about their circumstances.

C People stay inside because they fear the thunder.

D People are hot and miserable because there is no rain.

25 According to the poem, why is there no silence in the mountains?

A People are hoping for rain.

B People hear thunder in the distance.

C People are watching from their houses.

D People have gathered to wait for rain.

26 What does the poet **most likely** mean when he says "Dead mountain mouth of carious teeth that cannot spit" in line 13?

A People in the mountains are looking for water.

B The water in the mountains has dried up.

C People have no water in their mouths.

D The mountain is a lot like a person.

LANGUAGE AND LITERATURE: SESSION 3

This session contains two reading selections with thirteen multiple-choice questions and one open-response question. Mark your answers to these questions in the spaces provided on your Answer Sheet.

After the Civil War, there was no easy way to travel from east to west and vice versa. In 1869, the first railroad was built from coast to coast, making it easier for people to travel the entire country. Read the article "East Meets West" and answer the questions that follow.

East Meets West

1   Before the United States was even a hundred years old, it faced dilemmas that threatened to tear it to pieces. In the 1860s, the country endured the Civil War, which nearly ripped the northern states and southern states apart. During that time, there was also a great divide between the eastern and western territories. America's East and West were separated—not by war, but by distance and lack of transportation. As the Civil War was ending, a great innovation was chosen to pull the country back together: a railroad line that would reach from one end of the nation to the other.

2   In the 1800s, trains were a powerful and important means of transportation. People viewed these "iron horses" as awesome technology, much as we might view spaceships or jet planes today. Trains could move large amounts of people and cargo over land much more easily and effectively than horses or oxen could. Just as importantly, trains became a symbol to war-weary Americans. If railroad tracks could be built across the nation, they would unite the states and make America powerful again.

3   Today, in the age of spaceships and jets, this might seem an easy task. However, at the time, this was an extremely challenging feat. In the East, railroad tracks only reached as far as Nebraska. Meanwhile, in the West, railroads only ran north and south, making no attempt to connect with the East. There was a gap of about seventeen hundred miles between the eastern and western rail lines that kept the two halves of the nation apart.

4   Most people relied on wagon trains or long sea voyages to travel between the East and West. However, more and more people wanted to find another, more convenient way. A railroad would offer them a perfect opportunity. Investors and shopkeepers supported this idea because a railroad would help to encourage new towns full of potential buyers and sellers. Many investors and fortune hunters in the East were also excited to travel westward in search of gold.

5   Other Americans simply loved the idea of a new way to explore the country and learn about different places and ideas. In the 1800s, people did not have a complete picture of America because much of it was barely explored. In the cities of the East, people could only look at artists' paintings of the beauty of the West and guess at what it might look like in person. They wanted to see the prairies and the buffalo and the Sierra Nevada Mountains for themselves.

6   Many people wanted a railroad to be built, but nobody was sure who should build it. At first, the government and the army were set to carry the project through, but they both were hesitant. While they bickered among themselves, two private railroad companies took control of the project. These companies were the Union Pacific in the East and the Central Pacific in the West, and they became two of America's

Go On

most famous competitors. In 1866, Congress sanctioned these companies to begin laying track and work their way toward the middle of the country, where they would meet.

7   The Union Pacific, the eastern company, started the race first. They sent teams of scouts and engineers westward to sketch out the line that the railroad tracks would follow. Next, vast construction gangs were sent out to begin grading, or leveling, the land, often as much as a hundred miles at a time. After that came an army of track-laying crews, each made of ten thousand workers and as many animals. These crews had the enormous task of actually installing the railroad tracks, which required hundreds of tons of steel bars and timber ties. Although the Union Pacific teams were huge, they were able to work quickly and cover a lot of space. This was because most of the land in the East was flat, and because it was easy to get supplies from nearby cities.

8   The Central Pacific, working in the West, had neither of these benefits. Their terrain was much harsher, largely consisting of forests and mountains. Every mile presented new challenges, and the company spent years tunneling and bridging its way across the hilly land. Additionally, the Central Pacific had a difficult time getting supplies. They had enough timber locally, but all the steel rails and other materials (including the trains themselves) had to be shipped by sea.

9   The workforces of both the Union Pacific and the Central Pacific were largely made up of immigrants to America. The Union Pacific's team was almost entirely Irish immigrants, and the Central Pacific mostly hired Asians. These workers suffered greatly during the construction of the railroads, often fainting from the heat of prairie summers or freezing in the cold western mountains.

10   As the project went on, company officials demanded more and more labor from their workers for the sake of profit. The companies were making many thousands of dollars per mile of rail, and with all of the miles between the East and West, the moneymaking potential was almost endless. Even when the construction teams had almost met, they were instructed to lay tracks parallel to one another in order to cover more precious miles.

11   Finally, on May 10, 1869, the workers of the Union Pacific and Central Pacific met in Utah at a place they called Promontory Point. They had laid 1,775 miles of track over the course of over three years of hard labor. Finally, they could connect the tracks. Company officials and politicians raced to Promontory Point to hold ceremonies and celebrations. Bands and parades ushered in the new age for America, and five states donated golden and silver railroad spikes to be hammered into the rails to finish the project. The governor of California, Leland Stanford, pounded in the final, golden spike, and the news spread across America that the East and West had finally been united.

 What type of organization is used in paragraph 5?

A   definition

B   narration

C   cause and effect

D   comparison and contrast

 According to the article, what was the **main** advantage of railways compared with wagon trains or long sea voyages?

A   Railways were less expensive.

B   Railways were safer.

C   Railways were more convenient.

D   Railways were more exciting.

Go On

29 What is the **best** meaning of the word *sanctioned* as it is used in paragraph 6?

A punished

B gave permission

C denied rights

D examined ability

30 Which of the following is the **best** synonym for *ripped* as it is used in paragraph 1?

A disconnected

B torn

C moved

D broken

31 According to the article, which of these reasons contributed **most** to the slowness of the Central Pacific's progress?

A The government did not support the Central Pacific's work.

B The Central Pacific did not have enough timber to make rail ties.

C Less money was being offered to Central Pacific owners.

D Much of the Central Pacific's route was full of forests and mountains.

32 What is the author's purpose in writing this article?

A to describe what life was like for an immigrant worker in the 1860s

B to convince readers that the Civil War damaged America's sense of unity

C to inform readers about the history of one of America's great construction projects

D to explain why Promontory Point was chosen as the meeting point for railroads

33 Based on the article, why were workers from the competing rail lines instructed to lay tracks parallel to one another?

A It made the task of grading the land easier.

B It assured that the tracks would be straight.

C It would help travelers get to their destinations faster.

D It allowed railroad owners to be paid for extra miles.

34 Which of the following **best** summarizes paragraph 9?

A The immigrants froze when they worked during the winter months.

B The Union Pacific's team was filled with Irish immigrants.

C The immigrants hired to build the railroads suffered greatly.

D The Central Pacific mostly hired Asian Americans to build railroads.

Go On

Write your answer to open-response question 35 in the space provided on your Answer Sheet.

35 Explain the organizational pattern the author uses at the beginning of the article. Use relevant and specific information from the article to support your answer.

Henrik Ibsen (1826–1906) was a playwright whose most famous works depict strong women inhibited by the constraints of society. Read this excerpt from Ibsen's A Doll House *and answer the questions that follow.*

Excerpt from *A Doll's House*

by **Henrik Ibsen**

In this scene, Nora Helmer is confronted by a man named Nils Krogstad, from whom she illegally and secretly borrowed money to pay for a trip to help her ill husband, Torvald. Over the years, Nora has worked hard and saved to pay back the money to Krogstad, and the loan is almost fully repaid. However, Torvald is Krogstad's boss at the bank and has been considering firing Krogstad from his post.

1   KROGSTAD (*controlling himself*): Listen to me, Mrs. Helmer. If necessary, I am prepared to fight for my small post in the Bank as if I were fighting for my life.

NORA: So it seems.

KROGSTAD: It is not only for the sake of the money; indeed, that weighs least with me in the matter. There is another reason—well, I may as well tell you. My position is this. I daresay you know, like everybody else, that once, many years ago, I was guilty of an indiscretion.

NORA: I think I have heard something of the kind.

5   KROGSTAD: The matter never came into court; but every way seemed to be closed to me after that. So I took to the business that you know of. I had to do something; and, honestly, don't think I've been one of the worst. But now I must cut myself free from all that. My sons are growing up; for their sake I must try and win back as much respect as I can in the town. This post in the Bank was like the first step up for me—and now your husband is going to kick me downstairs again into the mud.

NORA: But you must believe me, Mr. Krogstad; it is not in my power to help you at all.

KROGSTAD: Then it is because you haven't the will; but I have means to compel you.

NORA: You don't mean that you will tell my husband that I owe you money?

KROGSTAD: Hm!—suppose I were to tell him?

10   NORA: It would be perfectly infamous of you. (*Sobbing.*) To think of his learning my secret, which has been my joy and pride, in such an ugly, clumsy way—that he should learn it from you! And it would put me in a horribly disagreeable position—

KROGSTAD: Only disagreeable?

NORA (*impetuously*): Well, do it, then!—and it will be the worse for you. My husband will see for himself what a blackguard you are, and you certainly won't keep your post then.

KROGSTAD: I asked you if it was only a disagreeable scene at home that you were afraid of?

NORA: If my husband does get to know of it, of course he will at once pay you what is still owing, and we shall have nothing more to do with you.

15   KROGSTAD (*coming a step nearer*): Listen to me, Mrs. Helmer. Either you have a very bad memory or you know very little of business. I shall be obliged to remind you of a few details.

Go On

NORA: What do you mean?

KROGSTAD: When your husband was ill, you came to me to borrow two hundred and fifty pounds.

NORA: I didn't know any one else to go to.

KROGSTAD: I promised to get you that amount—

20   NORA: Yes, and you did so.

KROGSTAD: I promised to get you that amount, on certain conditions. Your mind was so taken up with your husband's illness, and you were so anxious to get the money for your journey, that you seem to have paid no attention to the conditions of our bargain. Therefore it will not be amiss if I remind you of them. Now, I promised to get the money on the security of a bond which I drew up.

NORA: Yes, and which I signed.

KROGSTAD: Good. But below your signature there were a few lines constituting your father a surety for the money; those lines your father should have signed.

NORA: Should? He did sign them.

25   KROGSTAD: I had left the date blank; that is to say your father should himself have inserted the date on which he signed the paper. Do you remember that?

NORA: Yes, I think I remember—

KROGSTAD: Then I gave you the bond to send by post to your father. Is that not so?

NORA: Yes.

KROGSTAD: And you naturally did so at once, because five or six days afterwards you brought me the bond with your father's signature. And then I gave you the money.

30   NORA: Well, haven't I been paying it off regularly?

KROGSTAD: Fairly so, yes. But—to come back to the matter in hand—that must have been a very trying time for you, Mrs. Helmer?

NORA: It was, indeed.

KROGSTAD: Your father was very ill, wasn't he?

NORA: He was very near his end.

35   KROGSTAD: And died soon afterwards?

NORA: Yes.

KROGSTAD: Tell me, Mrs. Helmer, can you by any chance remember what day your father died?— on what day of the month, I mean.

NORA: Papa died on the 29th of September.

KROGSTAD: That is correct; I have ascertained it for myself. And, as that is so, there is a discrepancy (*taking a paper from his pocket*) which I cannot account for.

40   NORA: What discrepancy? I don't know—

KROGSTAD: The discrepancy consists, Mrs. Helmer, in the fact that your father signed this bond three days after his death.

NORA: What do you mean? I don't understand—

Go On

KROGSTAD: Your father died on the 29th of September. But, look here; your father dated his signature the 2nd of October. It is a discrepancy, isn't it? (*Nora is silent.*) Can you explain it to me? (*Nora is still silent.*) It is a remarkable thing, too, that the words "2nd of October," as well as the year, are not written in your father's handwriting but in one that I think I know. Well, of course it can be explained; your father may have forgotten to date his signature, and someone else may have dated it haphazard before they knew of his death. There is no harm in that. It all depends on the signature of the name; and that is genuine, I suppose, Mrs. Helmer? It was your father himself who signed his name here?

NORA (*after a short pause, throws her head up and looks defiantly at him*): No, it was not. It was I that wrote papa's name.

45   KROGSTAD: Are you aware that is a dangerous confession?

NORA: In what way? You shall have your money soon.

KROGSTAD: Let me ask you a question; why did you not send the paper to your father?

NORA: It was impossible; papa was so ill. If I had asked him for his signature, I should have had to tell him what the money was to be used for; and when he was so ill himself I couldn't tell him that my husband's life was in danger—it was impossible.

KROGSTAD: It would have been better for you if you had given up your trip abroad.

50   NORA: No, that was impossible. That trip was to save my husband's life; I couldn't give that up.

KROGSTAD: But did it never occur to you that you were committing a fraud on me?

NORA: I couldn't take that into account; I didn't trouble myself about you at all. I couldn't bear you, because you put so many heartless difficulties in my way, although you knew what a dangerous condition my husband was in.

KROGSTAD: Mrs. Helmer, you evidently do not realise clearly what it is that you have been guilty of. But I can assure you that my one false step, which lost me all my reputation, was nothing more or nothing worse than what you have done.

NORA: You? Do you ask me to believe that you were brave enough to run a risk to save your wife's life.

55   KROGSTAD: The law cares nothing about motives.

NORA: Then it must be a very foolish law.

KROGSTAD: Foolish or not, it is the law by which you will be judged, if I produce this paper in court.

NORA: I don't believe it. Is a daughter not to be allowed to spare her dying father anxiety and care? Is a wife not to be allowed to save her husband's life? I don't know much about law; but I am certain that there must be laws permitting such things as that. Have you no knowledge of such laws—you who are a lawyer? You must be a very poor lawyer, Mr. Krogstad.

KROGSTAD: Maybe. But matters of business—such business as you and I have had together—do you think I don't understand that? Very well. Do as you please. But let me tell you this—if I lose my position a second time, you shall lose yours with me. (*He bows, and goes out through the hall.*)

60   NORA (*appears buried in thought for a short time, then tosses her head*). Nonsense! Trying to frighten me like that!—I am not so silly as he thinks. (*Begins to busy herself putting the children's things in order.*) And yet—? No, it's impossible! I did it for love's sake.

Go On

36 According to the excerpt, why does Krogstad come to see Nora?

A He wants Nora to help him keep his job.

B He wants Nora to finish repaying her debt.

C He wants Nora to get a job at the bank.

D He wants Nora to tell her husband the truth.

37 In this excerpt, why does the author use dashes in several places?

A to indicate words that are not heard

B to indicate actions that are not spoken

C to indicate shifts in topic

D to indicate a change in speaker

38 In line 39, what does the word *discrepancy* mean?

A continuity

B diplomacy

C inconsistency

D strategy

39 Which word **best** describes Krogstad?

A sarcastic

B defensive

C confused

D cunning

40 According to the excerpt, why is Krogstad determined to keep his job?

A It pays a great deal of money.

B It earns him respect in the town.

C It offers him new challenges every day.

D It gives him a purpose in life.

Stop

ANSWERS

Composition

WRITING PROMPT SAMPLE ANSWER

In *Pride and Prejudice*, the character of Caroline Bingley is set up as the complete opposite of the main character, Elizabeth Bennet. Elizabeth is the daughter of a poor, country gentleman whereas Caroline is a wealthy heiress. Both of the young women are proud, but their pride stems from different sources. Caroline's pride is the result of having fine things and being a member of high society, while Elizabeth's pride is the result of being independent and speaking her mind. Throughout the novel, the differences between these two women are highlighted. One example of this can be seen in the beginning of the book when Elizabeth walks three miles to Netherfield to see her ill sister, Jane. When she arrives, her hair is messy and the bottom of her dress is covered in dirt. Caroline tells her brother and Mr. Darcy how wild she thinks Elizabeth looks and says that she doesn't think a lady should walk so far unaccompanied. Elizabeth doesn't seem to care what anyone thinks about her behavior and only cares to attend to her sister. From this example, it is easy to see that appearance is very important to Caroline, while it does not seem to matter that much to Elizabeth.

LANGUAGE AND LITERATURE

1   C   Standard 13

While answer choice B might seem to be correct, the article does not really present the history of the *Arabia*; it tells about the Hawleys and how they discovered the *Arabia*. Therefore, answer choice C is the best answer.

2   B   Standard 8

To correctly answer this question, you need to apply what you have learned about the Hawleys. They looked at an old map to see where a river used to run.

3   A   Standard 8

Buried boats are often undiscovered because changes in rivers and nearby land have caused the sunken ships to be where people would not normally look.

4   A   Standard 8

The answer to this question is right in the article. When the Hawleys began digging, they were surprised to discover water.

5   Sample answer   Standard 13

According to the article, the treasures the Hawleys found inside the buried *Arabia* included everything from fine silk to canned goods. These materials had been somewhat preserved in the cool, damp mud. However, the Hawleys knew that by removing them from this environment, they would quickly dry out and begin to rot. In order to prevent the materials from deteriorating, they stabilized them by soaking and freezing them and then coating them in wax. By treating the materials this way, they could keep them as relics from history.

6   C   Standard 13

Often, as in this case, the correct answer to a question like this one is the most general. The best summary of paragraph 14 is answer choice C: the Hawleys took care to preserve the artifacts they found on the *Arabia*.

7   A   Standard 8

Answer choices B, C, and D are all supporting details found in the passage. Only answer choice A explains what the whole passage is about: two men who discovered the *Arabia*.

8   B   Standard 12

If the answer to this question is not obvious to you, you can find it through process of elimination. The author is not really concerned about sunken ships; he certainly is not indifferent because he cares that they are found, and he is not suspicious.

9   Sample answer   Standard 8

According to the article, the Hawleys learned about the *Arabia* while reading an old newspaper. The article said the ship sank in a river a mile below a town named Parksville. The Hawleys were able to locate Parksville but not the river. Then David Hawley found an old map of the town and discovered there was once a river where the ship sank. The brothers drew up a new map and, with the permission of farmers who now owned the land, they went into the cornfields with metal detectors. The metal detectors located the engines and boilers of the ship. Then they built irrigation wells and constructed water pumps to drain the water they found underneath the land. After nearly five months, they sighted the sunken ship.

10   C   Standard 14

Lines 17 and 18 from the poem mean that the speaker of the poem is hurt not by her relationship's ending but by the way it ended, over little things. Answer choice C is the best answer.

11   D   Standard 14

Although answer choice A might seem correct, in the beginning of the poem, the speaker is remembering a happy time. Answer choice D is the best answer.

12   B   Standard 14

In line 11 of the poem, the speaker says that her love laughed at everything she liked.

13   C   Standard 14

The poet is sad, but she is not angry or bitter. The mood is not really peaceful, nor is it entirely lighthearted.

14   D   Standard 5

The rubber plant's view of what is happening is very humorous. Answer choice D is the best answer.

15   C   Standard 8

The rubber plant says that the young girl lives in a decent place and puts him in a window. She seems to treat him nicely, but he says she is not his style because she is "too quiet and sober looking."

16   B   Standard 8

The excerpt says that Miss Caruthers's friend left him with her things, which were taken to a second-hand store.

17   A   Standard 4

In paragraph 5, the rubber plant says he was grouped with Henry James' works, six talking machine records, one pair of tennis shoes, and two bottles of horse radish. This is a very odd combination.

18   B   Standard 8

The rubber plant says several times that his first owners were a lot of fun.

19   A   Standard 12

The rubber plant's description of the girl making music is not pretty or nice; she probably wasn't very good.

20   B   Standard 12

The rubber plant doesn't think that they could stand under a rubber plant. He thinks they are exaggerating or lying.

21   D   Standard 8

The girl thinks the rubber plant is a magnolia, which gives the story a humorous ending.

22   Standard 11

The rubber plant records the stories of people's lives by watching what happens and judging them. He likes the people who ate lobster and had a lot of fun. He does not like it when the girl cries over him, and he enjoys it when people's lives are interesting and fun for him to watch.

23   A   Standard 14

The people in the poem are hot and desperate for water or rain that does not seem to be coming.

24   D   Standard 14

People are upset because there is no rain. Answer choice D is the best answer.

25   B   Standard 14

Lines 20 and 21 of the poem say that there is no silence in the mountains because of the thunder.

26   B   Standard 14

The poet is personifying the mountains, where there is no water.

27   B   Standard 5

The author simply tells the story in paragraph 5. He is using narration.

28   C   Standard 8

The article says in paragraph 4 that people wanted trains mainly because they would be a more convenient way to travel.

29   B   Standard 4

You have to look at the context of this word to correctly answer the question. In paragraph 6, the author says that Congress *sanctioned* these companies to begin laying track, which means that Congress gave them the go-ahead.

30   A   Standard 4

Paragraph 1 says that the Civil War nearly ripped the United States in half; in this case, *ripped* means *disconnected*.

31   D   Standard 8

The answer to this question is given in paragraph 8.

32   C   Standard 13

While answer choice D might seem to be correct, most of the article is not about Promontory Point. Answer choice C is the best answer.

33   D   Standard 8

You can find the answer to this question in paragraph 10.

34   C   Standard 13

Paragraph 9 is mainly about the way in which the immigrants who built the tracks suffered. Because both the Union Pacific and the Central Pacific hired immigrants, you can eliminate answer choices B and D. Answer choice A might seem correct, but it only explains one group of immigrant workers. In reality, both groups suffered greatly.

35   Sample answer   Standard 5

The author begins the article about the railroads in the United States by giving some history. In paragraph 1, the author explains that there was a great divide between the East and West because people had no way to travel from one end of the country to the other. They relied mainly on pictures and learn what the other side of the country looked like. Organizing the article in this manner helps readers understand the need for the railroad.

36 A Standard 11

Krogstad comes to see Nora to blackmail her so he won't be fired.

37 C Standard 5

The conversation between Nora and Krogstad is tense; the author uses the dashes to show that the topic of their conversation changes quickly. Both characters seem to try to think ahead.

38 C Standard 4

In line 39, Krogstad points out that the dates on the document are not consistent. This is the discrepancy.

39 D Standard 13

Krogstad has many characteristics, but he is mainly cunning.

40 B Standard 8

In line 5, Krogstad explains that he mainly wants respect.

Composition

SESSION 1

1 Ⓐ Ⓑ Ⓒ Ⓓ   **2** Ⓐ Ⓑ Ⓒ Ⓓ   **3** Ⓐ Ⓑ Ⓒ Ⓓ

4 Ⓐ Ⓑ Ⓒ Ⓓ   **5** Ⓐ Ⓑ Ⓒ Ⓓ   **6** Ⓐ Ⓑ Ⓒ Ⓓ

7 Ⓐ Ⓑ Ⓒ Ⓓ   **8** Ⓐ Ⓑ Ⓒ Ⓓ

9 _____

_____

_____

10 Ⓐ Ⓑ Ⓒ Ⓓ   **11** Ⓐ Ⓑ Ⓒ Ⓓ   **12** Ⓐ Ⓑ Ⓒ Ⓓ

13 Ⓐ Ⓑ Ⓒ Ⓓ   **14** Ⓐ Ⓑ Ⓒ Ⓓ   **15** Ⓐ Ⓑ Ⓒ Ⓓ

16 Ⓐ Ⓑ Ⓒ Ⓓ   **17** Ⓐ Ⓑ Ⓒ Ⓓ

SESSION 2

18 _____

_____

_____

19 Ⓐ Ⓑ ⓒ Ⓓ   **20** Ⓐ Ⓑ ⓒ Ⓓ   **21** Ⓐ Ⓑ ⓒ Ⓓ

22 Ⓐ Ⓑ ⓒ Ⓓ   **23** Ⓐ Ⓑ ⓒ Ⓓ   **24** Ⓐ Ⓑ ⓒ Ⓓ

25 Ⓐ Ⓑ ⓒ Ⓓ   **26** Ⓐ Ⓑ ⓒ Ⓓ

27 _____

_____

_____

SESSION 3

28 Ⓐ Ⓑ ⓒ Ⓓ   **29** Ⓐ Ⓑ ⓒ Ⓓ   **30** Ⓐ Ⓑ ⓒ Ⓓ

32 Ⓐ Ⓑ ⓒ Ⓓ   **33** Ⓐ Ⓑ ⓒ Ⓓ   **34** Ⓐ Ⓑ ⓒ Ⓓ

35 Ⓐ Ⓑ ⓒ Ⓓ

36 _____

_____

_____

37 Ⓐ Ⓑ ⓒ Ⓓ   **38** Ⓐ Ⓑ ⓒ Ⓓ   **39** Ⓐ Ⓑ ⓒ Ⓓ

40 Ⓐ Ⓑ ⓒ Ⓓ

Composition

SESSION 1

1 Ⓐ Ⓑ Ⓒ Ⓓ   **2** Ⓐ Ⓑ Ⓒ Ⓓ   **3** Ⓐ Ⓑ Ⓒ Ⓓ

4 Ⓐ Ⓑ Ⓒ Ⓓ

5 _____

_____

_____

6 Ⓐ Ⓑ Ⓒ Ⓓ   **7** Ⓐ Ⓑ Ⓒ Ⓓ   **8** Ⓐ Ⓑ Ⓒ Ⓓ

9 _____

_____

_____

10 Ⓐ Ⓑ Ⓒ Ⓓ   **11** Ⓐ Ⓑ Ⓒ Ⓓ   **12** Ⓐ Ⓑ Ⓒ Ⓓ

13 Ⓐ Ⓑ Ⓒ Ⓓ   **14** Ⓐ Ⓑ Ⓒ Ⓓ   **15** Ⓐ Ⓑ Ⓒ Ⓓ

16 Ⓐ Ⓑ Ⓒ Ⓓ   **17** Ⓐ Ⓑ Ⓒ Ⓓ   **18** Ⓐ Ⓑ Ⓒ Ⓓ

SESSION 2

19 Ⓐ Ⓑ Ⓒ Ⓓ   **20** Ⓐ Ⓑ Ⓒ Ⓓ   **21** Ⓐ Ⓑ Ⓒ Ⓓ

22 _____

_____

_____

23 Ⓐ Ⓑ Ⓒ Ⓓ   **24** Ⓐ Ⓑ Ⓒ Ⓓ   **25** Ⓐ Ⓑ Ⓒ Ⓓ

26 Ⓐ Ⓑ Ⓒ Ⓓ

Session 3

27 Ⓐ Ⓑ Ⓒ Ⓓ   **28** Ⓐ Ⓑ Ⓒ Ⓓ   **29** Ⓐ Ⓑ Ⓒ Ⓓ

30 Ⓐ Ⓑ Ⓒ Ⓓ   **32** Ⓐ Ⓑ Ⓒ Ⓓ   **33** Ⓐ Ⓑ Ⓒ Ⓓ

34 Ⓐ Ⓑ Ⓒ Ⓓ

35 _____

_____

_____

36 Ⓐ Ⓑ Ⓒ Ⓓ   **37** Ⓐ Ⓑ Ⓒ Ⓓ   **38** Ⓐ Ⓑ Ⓒ Ⓓ

39 Ⓐ Ⓑ Ⓒ Ⓓ   **40** Ⓐ Ⓑ Ⓒ Ⓓ

Index

Photo Credits

"The Six Nations of the Iroquois" (p. 5) courtesy New York Public Library.

"Curious Crop Circles (p. 12) by ©iStockphoto.com/George Cairns.

"The Coolest Invention" (p. 40) courtesy Carrier Corporation.

"The Thinking Spot" (p. 43) by ©iStockphoto.com/Jan Ball.

"Superstition Mission" (p. 56) by ©iStockphoto.com/Jaimie D. Travis.

"I Wandered Lonely as a Child," daffodils image (p. 77) by ©iStockphoto.com/Bill Storage.

"Se-Osirus and the Sealed Scroll," image of Ramses (p. 89) by ©iStockphoto.com/Vladimir Pomortsev.

"Tarantula Tamer" (p. 110) by ©iStockphoto.com/David Haynes.

NOTES

NOTES